Praise for

The Wrong Son

"In lesser hands, this story of overwhelming grief, pain, loss, and personal chaos would be too much for the reader to bear, but Neil Griffiths has managed to take the harrowing stuff of his life that is near impossible to put down. An incredible achievement." —Erin Vincent, *Fourteen Ways of Looking*

"Simply put, I could not leave it alone. Neil Griffiths has written something profoundly honest, and transparently so, which is partly what makes it so compelling, and also something that comes from a place of deep understanding, gleaned carefully over many years of a life lived thoughtfully. He has achieved something wonderful." —Marina Benjamin, *A Little Give*

"I'm pleased, if that's the word, that the author of *The Wrong Son* has been able to write this book. His memoir is the story of a family ghosted by lives and loves cut short. It's also a brilliant summoning of the feeling of the 70s – class pride and aspiration in deep conflict. Many of the incidents, the humiliations, are shocking (we still balk at the idea of parents not liking their children) but relayed with a compassionate sense of how that shockingness only reveals itself at a much later date, how the meaning keeps unfolding. So many families are so strange, though nothing is strange to life, of course. And nothing about this superb account feels unfair or forced. It is a case study of misdirected emotions, and the best thing Neil Griffiths has written." —Will Eaves, *Murmur*

"In this incredibly moving, refreshingly self-critical memoir, in succinct and elegant prose Griffiths eviscerates his personal history. For all its hard truth, shattering emotion and psychoanalysis, *The Wrong Son* is a strangely propulsive, absorbing read." —Sara Baume, *Seven Steeples*

"*The Wrong Son* combines the page-turning quality of the best fiction with the astute self-awareness of the best memoir. Neil Griffiths, a master storyteller, characterises himself as furious and faulted, as well as vulnerable, in this moving, funny, dark and psychologically fascinating exploration of what it means to be born to a couple blinded by tragedy and grief. I loved this memoir's humility and admired its courage." —Lily Dunn, *Sins of My Father*

"Neil Griffiths has written an existential ghost story reminiscent of the finest screenplays. Reading *The Wrong Son*, I was reminded of Hitchcock's *Shadow of a Doubt* and the figure of the familial imposter haunting the lives of the living and the dead; the uncanny character wreaking havoc over the noble efforts of young lives desperately trying to remain intact. In lean, eviscerating prose, Griffiths shows how the bludgeoning dramas of the past threaten to deform the chance at a real self. An unflinching self-examination in the tradition of Dostoyevsky's Raskolnikov." —Sally Bayley, *No Boys Play Here*

"A brilliant anatomy of a deeply wounding childhood, *The Wrong Son* is both heartbreaking and profoundly moving in its honesty and humanity. Griffiths has wrested from his own anguish and confusion a clear-eyed portrait of the dark legacy of repressed grief and the agony of every child who yearns for the love of an emotionally unavailable and abusive parent." —Rebecca Abrams, *When Parents Die*

"*The Wrong Son* is a haunting, visceral memoir recounting a disaster, a child born in the wrong place, the wrong time. Written with emotional precision, deftly braided with psycho-analytical theory, we witness a life emerging in loss, violence and the alienating absence of love: a son growing up with Winnicott's tenet: It is a joy to be hidden and a disaster not to be found. The story exhumes parenthood, grief, and our ineluctable human longing for love. Griffiths has achieved a mighty feat, for *The Wrong Son* is also endlessly compulsive and funny, while asking the fundamental question of how we exist. This book is here to stay." —Susanna Crossman, *Home is Where We Start*

THE WRONG SON

Neil Griffiths

WEATHERGLASS BOOKS

THE WRONG SON

For Dorothy (1933–1962)

&

Michael (1960–1962)

&

Toni

'[It is] like a man who has an unsafe house and wants to build himself a safe one beside it, using the materials of the old one if possible. But it's a terrible business if, during construction, his strength wanes and now instead of an unsafe but whole house, he has one that's half torn down and one that's half built, which is nothing. What follows is madness, a kind of Cossack dance between the two houses, during which the Cossack scrapes and hollows out the ground with the heels of his boots until his own grave takes shape beneath him.'

from Franz Kafka's Notebooks

Part One

-2–0 Years Old

October 1963

My father is driving home to suburban London from Dover, on the Kent coast, after a row with his mother at a family gathering. In the car with him is his first wife, Dorothy, seven months pregnant, and their two-year-old son, Michael. My father's mother is difficult; she likes to cause trouble between her six children, play them off against one another, mostly by privileging my father, the firstborn, often treating him as an only child, as if she'd given birth to something special, a misplaced prince who requires homage, devotion, exclusive love.

The family gathering was for a birthday, but also because his father is unwell. He will soon be diagnosed with lung cancer. Every photograph of him has a cigarette hanging between his lips: a short, stocky, pale, craggy Humphrey Bogart. A quiet man before the war, he was almost silent afterwards. As with many families, certain foundational stories remain vague: a merchant seaman, he went missing for several months and was presumed dead. I heard this story told by my grandmother and aunts. The Dover accent has a twang, the women's voices tend to huskiness, and if they smoke, when they laugh, it sounds as if their lungs are rattling. To my father it sounded brash, gossipy, unruly; you could see him lean away in their company.

What the family row was about remains a mystery, but my father wasn't a man to make a scene. Dorothy would have read the situation and known what to do. And what to expect when they were in the car. Silent fury.

An hour later they are nearing London. In the passenger seat Michael is playing on Dorothy's lap. Coming the other way at speed, on the wrong side of the road, for reasons we will never know, is another car.

Neither my father nor Dorothy is wearing a seat belt. As the two cars collide, my father is protected by the steering wheel and his big hand flat against the windscreen. Michael crashes through the windscreen and onto the bonnet. Dorothy, heavily pregnant, is crushed against the dashboard. The driver of the other car lives, his girlfriend dies.

These are the only details of The Accident, as it came to be known. An accident like this would still make the national news today.

Ten days later, my father wakes from a coma in Orpington Hospital. His wife and child are dead, already buried in a churchyard in Grantham, Lincolnshire. This is where Dorothy is from, where she and my father met during his national service. Dorothy is the only child of elderly parents. They are broken by her death and never fully recover. I don't know why the funeral was arranged so quickly.

My father comes to without any memory of what happened. His jaw is wired shut, and stitches on his right palm keep two jagged cuts closed. The cuts will leave thick, livid scarring. Years later, when I ask him about these, he'll say he got them in the war. Throughout the rest of his life, at times of stress he will have nightmares, reliving what he can't remember. Every October he will become ill for a week.

As the story goes, hours or days before The Accident, but not long before, my father is standing in his garden after a day's work, a cold drink in his hand, at which point he feels an overwhelming sense of contentment. He has everything he wants: a wife, a young son, another child on the way; he owns his home, keeps a few ducks in the garden, the summer has been full of cricket. Maybe Dorothy calls him in for dinner, or it's time for the evening news, but he will go inside the house, disappearing into the humdrum of married life in the early 1960s. Except that shortly afterwards – at this point it doesn't matter how much time passes – his family is dead, and he decides forevermore that he will never again let himself feel this kind of contentment. Or so the story goes.

My maternal great-grandmother died of Spanish flu in 1918 when my grandmother, Isobel, was a child. This was in Scotland, in the mining village of Blantyre, a place unchanged from the eighteenth century, with single-room cottages, an open fire, nooks carved into the walls for sleeping. Isobel grew into a small, abrasive, stern woman, distrustful of affection. At seventeen she married a man she'd only known three weeks. The wedding took place in a social club along with twenty other couples, all chanting their vows with, I suspect, varying degrees of enthusiasm. There was no dancing. My grandparents' honeymoon was the journey south to London, to Surbiton, where they lived in the same flat for the rest of their lives. Like the cottage my grandmother had left, their new flat had no bathroom; instead, a large tin tub hung on the wall of the steep back stairs. Isobel worked as a washerwoman in a nursery, where up until the 1970s children slept in beds twice a day. My grandfather, George, was a painter and decorator. In all the photographs of him he has a cigarette between his knuckles: a pleasant, pale, red-haired, open-faced Stan Laurel. He didn't speak much, except to intone 'Ah, it's terrible' at odd moments, letting those around him know that he knew the world for what it was. Like my paternal grandfather, he was dying of lung cancer by his mid-sixties. Isobel nursed him at home until his death. I remember her carrying him in her arms from the bed to the tin tub, both tiny and bent, a blend of limbs. I was staying there for a short while and watched through the door. It was a sunny August day when he died. I prevented my mother being there by making some demand of her; I cannot remember what it was.

Although she always said she felt Scottish, my mother was born in London. She remembered the Blitz, huddling in the cupboard under the stairs with her little brother, her mother's cold grip on her shoulder, fingernails digging into her flesh.

At sixteen she was apprenticed to a hairdresser from Italy. That summer she and a friend travelled by train across Europe to Naples to his villa in Sorrento, its pale stone made bright by the sun; the house had a large swimming pool, and only a short walk away, down a steep set of rocks, was the sea, with Capri in the distance. This was

1952. Although she never did anything like this again, she went on to think of that trip as defining, insisting that the glamour said something fundamental about who she was, that if things had been different she might have lived the life of a character in an Italian movie. I remember her saying the names of Italian actresses, Gee-*na*-lo-*la*-brid-gid-*da*, Claudia *Car*-din-*are*-lay, the overpronouncing of their multisyllable names a declaration of her affinity with them. She said more than once that she had the right figure for an actress at that time.

Two years later, she meets and then marries her first husband, Ron, a gas fitter, five years older. He was a Teddy boy, and glamorous in the way Teddy boys are with their exaggerated Edwardian pomp. They moved into the ground-floor flat below her parents, a tin tub on the wall outside. A year or so later there was a baby daughter, Antoinette – Toni. From that moment on, my mother found herself unable to bear being touched by her husband.

After The Accident, my father slept on the kitchen table with his feet against the boiler. It was the only way, my mother said, he could wake up early enough for work, the boiler presumably on some sort of timer. My father's third wife, Anne, a devout Catholic, would later say he did it as a kind of penance: the hardness of the table, the burn of the hot metal on the soles of his feet. Both could be true, of course.

My father's terrible grief, my mother's frustrated life – they were going on a short distance apart.

In loving memory of Dorothy Christine aged 28 years and Michael Julian aged 2 years, who died in a road accident 26th of October 1962, the dear wife and only child of Michael Griffiths

Ghosts

Early spring 1963 and my mother is returning home after a trip to the shops. She notices a policeman on the other side of the road. He follows her from the high street, along the main road to where she lives. She stops and looks at him; he is very handsome. There is no acknowledgement of what's happening. He doesn't wave; she doesn't smile.

A week later, Thelma, my mother's next-door neighbour, says she wants to visit a newly demolished building in the hope of finding material for her rockery. Thelma is unusual for the time: she is married but has no children, and she can drive. She even has a car. My mother leaves Toni upstairs with her grandparents, and she and Thelma set off. They are in the car for less than two minutes when my mother begins to think they are being followed. She says she recognises the policeman from the week before. Thelma pulls over, the other car pulls over, and two men emerge. When windows are wound down my mother says, 'I saw you the other day, you followed me.' It is not denied. All they want, the two men say, is to go for a quick drink. Thelma is keen. My mother tells Thelma she wants to go home.

Ten minutes after this, they are sitting in the saloon bar of the nearest pub. Both men are policemen; they are off to play cricket close by. Do the women want to come and watch? My mother and Thelma laugh. They come from football-only households. At some point, when my father isn't present, the other man tells them about The Accident. My mother's first thought is that his son, had he still been alive, would be the same age as her daughter. She insists on being taken home.

Over the next weeks my father appears, sometimes in uniform, sometimes not – in which case they usually go for a drink. She thinks he might be the most handsome man she's ever seen. She decides she cannot think of which movie star he looks like because he looks like them all. The wounds on his right hand, the recent scarring, become a way of talking about what happened. My father's hands are large, his fingers shapeless, dumb, useless for intricate work, but they are expressive, commanding. He tells her about the hours or days before The Accident, his moment of contentment. He also says he now believes life owes him. It is a statement of fact. A warning.

Within three months, my mother has left Ron and Toni, and over the next sixteen years Toni's age, like Michael's, will be totted up from this sudden point of absence, the two ageing in ghostly parallel.

Ghosts are difficult to observe and pin down. To live in a house of ghosts from the beginning of one's life, it becomes necessary to ignore them, to make them doubly invisible. But they cannot be escaped. Jacques Derrida described the persistence of elements of the social or cultural past as 'hauntology'. Surely the term is better deployed as the study of individuals being a product of ghosts. In this sense, I would make a good case study.

Fifty years on, my mother says, 'What kind of mother leaves her child?' I don't think 'kind' is right – there are no categories. Perhaps, I say, it started with her grandmother dying of Spanish flu: a young child loses her mother, a bond is suddenly broken, the child then becomes a mother whose bond with her own daughter is perhaps not sufficiently strong because of her own experience of rupture and then … I shrug.

There are times when I see my mother transform into her mother, especially when warmth is required of her, or gratitude, or even an acknowledgement that someone has thought of her, such as a well-chosen present. Her face hardens; she withdraws. I also don't like to receive presents; I don't know how to accept them, as if they contain a meaning I can't fathom.

It is not odd that my father would pursue a new partner when he did; a six-month gap is broadly in line with the research around widowers at the time. But knowing the kind of man he was, I do wonder why, at a time when a police officer having an affair was a sackable offence, he chose a married woman with a child, with the inevitable emotional complications, the professional risk. The only answer I can offer is that my father had a highly attuned instinct for women who would look after him, predict his moods and attend to him with silent activity, and when he encountered one he went after her. If my mother is to be believed, he chose her from across the road that first afternoon.

My mother and father find places to spend the afternoon together. For my mother, it involves leaving Toni with her grandparents, or with Thelma. It involves deceit and abandonment, terrible guilt. But also excitement: a sense of life becoming something she recognises as due to her – the life of a movie star in all its intrigue. My father's friends tell her he is much in demand: their mothers send daughters to cook for him, who return in a swoon. But still he pursues this married woman with a two-year-old child. It is for this reason that she believes she must be special.

What does it feel like when they are in bed together? No doubt there are times where no one else exists, not the little girl, the dead family. They are living in the present. What do they talk about? The same as all lovers? Possibility and impossibility are at that moment exquisitely the same thing.

At one point they are discovered. It's a scene from a comedy. Ron runs down the street shouting, 'My wife's in bed with that policeman!' My grandmother goes down to the police station and says to the officer at the desk, 'Tell that policeman to leave my daughter alone.' My grandmother was a small, fierce, bony woman. When she spoke, the movement of her false teeth gave her a kind of vehemence, as if she might take a bite out of you and leave the teeth in your arm. I was terrified of her. The police took no action. His recent bereavement may have meant his offence was overlooked.

A few weeks into the affair, my mother discovers she is pregnant. It is Ron's. How she knows this, I don't know.

Timing; contraception? Huddled in the corner of a pub, looking around as if they might have been followed, she tells my father as if she is sharing a terrible secret that will ruin everything. He is irritated: he can't disguise this, but he knows what can be done, if she is willing. I wonder how this felt at the time. A test of their love or a sign that it was time to give up?

Abortions are still illegal in 1963, but as a police officer my father knows a woman. My mother goes alone on the bus. The procedure involves injecting a soapy solution via the vagina into the womb, after which the woman is sent home to await the foetus's evacuation, usually into a toilet, to be flushed away. With both her parents at work, my mother plans to go to their flat, up the steep stairs from where she lives, where she can be alone all afternoon. The cramps begin on the bus, and she fears the foetus will slip out. She uses the extra padding she has been given, wraps both arms around her abdomen, clutches hard, breathes deeply like she remembers being told to when giving birth. The bus stop is at the end of her street. She needs the bus conductor to help her down onto the pavement. Bent over, hand on garden walls and front gates, the soapy solution mixed with blood running down the insides of her thighs, she makes it to the block of flats in stages and climbs the steep stairs on her hands and knees.

Such is the pain, my mother believes she is going to die, that she deserves to die because she's brought it all on herself. Sitting in the small toilet, hand pressed hard into her stomach – pushing the foetus down and out, she thinks – she regrets everything she's done and wills life to be as it was before she met my father. But only for an instant. She also promises herself that after this she will not go back to her old life, that like my father she is now owed something for all her suffering.

My mother made the first bargain because it seemed a terrible thing to have done and that she must be punished. But she also knew it was because she believed in a future with my father. No one, she reasons, has an abortion to make things worse, and so she must have done it for a good reason, and she needs to see it through and move on. She is narrowing down her old life into this single, terrible moment in the belief that once it is all over, a new life, full of possibility, will widen out in front of her.

My mother eventually leaves Ron and moves into a room in a friend's house, taking Toni with her. The friend looks after Toni while my mother is at work. Ron comes and takes Toni. My mother then takes her back when Ron is at work. This happens several times, at which point my mother flees to Scotland with Toni. To her relatives in Blantyre. They still live in the single room with its large open fire and nooks in the wall for sleeping.

Somehow my father finds out where she is and drives there. He is taller than the doorway and has to lean his head to one side when standing in the room. My mother says it was like the laird walking in, bigger because better fed, tall and straight for never having been down a mine. He doesn't raise his voice – a terrifying sound – but says my mother is to come with him now, this minute. What happens next happens fast: my mother finds herself in the car with Toni, her daughter's bib still on, food around her mouth, their belongings left behind.

My father takes my mother to live with his parents in Dover, to a small flat she claims was always shrouded in mist from the sea. He returns to London. She leaves everything behind: work, friends, and even Toni, who is returned to Ron. My father's four sisters, all now married with children, are suspicious of her. How is it this woman has left her child? No one speaks to her. She wanders the drab coastal town in tears, sits on the grey stones of the beach, looks out over the indifferent sea. At an agreed time each evening she finds a phone box and calls my father, jamming coins into the slot.

One evening she is too ill to get out of bed and doesn't call. That weekend, down from London, my father refuses to speak to her, turns his impressive physical presence into an obdurate, unchallengeable silence. My mother finds herself kneeling at his feet, promising it will never happen again, begging him to forgive her. Later she said it was then that she knew what pain he would cause her.

It isn't only my mother's love that keeps them together at this point, though. My father has driven to Scotland, eight hours there and back, placed her with his parents in Dover, drives down to see her every week. He is putting in the miles for something. For a man who likes an easy life, this requires a lot of hard work. The reason is simple: he loves her. And it's what we do when we love someone, isn't it?

When I talked to my mother about that time, it always seemed an impossible mixture of heartache and practicalities. As each day dawned, her heart broke for Toni, and yet each day steps were taken to build a new life. She was forced to split herself: to miss her daughter while at the same time being in love, full of hope. Was it the same for my father? I don't think a split was necessary: there wasn't any choice, there was no possibility of going back to an old life, no parallel life on offer, no others waiting who loved him. There was only the future.

It isn't long before my father puts in for a transfer to a different station and buys a two-bedroom bungalow with a large garden about twenty miles from my mother's old life. It is a new build, on an unmade road, with empty and half-built houses up and over a hill. Before they move in, my mother asks the question she has been unable to ask for weeks, fearing the answer.

'Can I bring Toni?'

Apparently my father says, 'You can, but I'd prefer it if you didn't.' There are different ways of reading this. Selfish, callous, cold. Or that he needed her be willing to lose everything too. To start again together. My mother tells herself Toni will be with a loving father, and as much as this hurts, it is for the best. For everyone. This is not quite true. Her husband wants his wife back, and her daughter wants her mother back. It is not best for them. It is not for the best for my mother, either: she wants her daughter with her.

It is no longer heartache my mother feels, that mixture of pain, yearning and hope. She is now broken-hearted. She now has to wake up in a new house, miles from her daughter, knowing that there was a second or two when she could have insisted things had to be different, that it could have been otherwise. She feels as if her insides are being scythed up. Some mornings it even feels like her child is dead. But she isn't: she is with her dad, in her home, her grandparents only a climb up the steep back stairs. However, the man lying next to her, the man she has chosen over her daughter, his child is dead.

To lose a child like that must feel like the world has been turned upside down. There is nothing worse. It's how it's spoken about: 'There is nothing worse than ...' A child's loss of a parent is a more common experience, divided up between a parent dying young (my great-grandmother) and a parent choosing a new life (my mother). To lose a child is worse, of course. But a child losing its parent to a choice made by that parent, deciding they wanted a different life – the child must live their whole life with the knowledge that they were not chosen.

Around this time, my parents talk about starting a family.

Objects

When my parents were having their first children, ideas about child development were beginning to change, particularly in Britain. Psychiatrist and psychoanalyst D. W. Winnicott wrote books for the general reader and spoke on the radio about the 'baby as a person', the 'good enough mother' and the 'transitional object'. But my parents didn't read, and the radio in their house was for music. They belonged to the last generation raised by Victorian parents, shaped by war, rationing, and the expectation that children were fed, clothed and most importantly 'seen but not heard'.

Broadly, my father sought a world of good manners and humility, and that started with children raised with discipline and boundaries set down by the father. If it included love, discipline and boundaries came first, after which love was then deserved, as a reward. All his life he would describe children as either 'trouble' or 'no trouble', a judgement he believed held for the rest of their lives. I know he recognised that some children had worse starts in life than others, but he looked to the upkeep of their homes: a clean and tidy home was an indication of good parenting; orderliness didn't happen by itself.

It's always been difficult to determine what my mother thought. It wasn't a subject she was easily drawn on, with often strange explanations like, 'I gave birth to you,' or, 'It never mattered what I thought.' Later in life she claimed to have done her best with what little she had, using her limited housekeeping money as a metaphor for something else that had been in short supply.

But whatever they thought of parenting generally, neither of them thought about how what they'd been through might affect a new baby – after all, what can a baby, infant, child know if they aren't told? They assumed that their grief and guilt stopped with them.

I should say here that I've been suspicious of psychoanalysis most of my life, and Freud is probably the only writer whose work I've ever wanted to throw across the room. Yet I've never been able to disabuse myself of his core belief that the self is fundamentally split: there are thoughts, behaviours, desires to which we are blind, and these often inform the nature of our most important relationships. At the time of my birth, my parents believed they'd been given a chance of a new beginning. There was nothing else going on.

There is a Chinese proverb: 'It can be difficult to find a black cat in a darkened room, especially when there is no black cat'. When it came to their plans, my mother and father would have said there was no black cat. For decades I agreed. Then my father died and all the lights came on and I saw it. A moment later they went out again and I was left in darkness, the black cat still somewhere in the room.

It was at this point that I needed help. At the time there was more chance it would have been finding God, given the novel I was working on at the time. But somehow I arrived at psychoanalysis. In terms of lighting the room, it was the object relations school of D. W. Winnicott and R. W. Fairbairn, but when it came to finding the black cat, it was Jacques Lacan.

There seemed to be something uncannily familiar about the work of these analysts. My recognition was instant. The comfort was instant. When reading Lacan I started to wonder whether he ever travelled over from Paris and looked in through our kitchen window, because so much of what he wrote about was being played out around the kitchen table. His theory of the *Nom-du-Père* (Name-of-the-Father) focused on how we come to negotiate a world of constraints and rules that have been in place long before our arrival and that we must learn to abide by. He later generalised the concept as the 'paternal function'. What matters is not the content of the paternal function itself, but how the primary caregiver presents it to the infant. And so I suppose my question is: what becomes of the infant if the paternal function is presented as *infallible* and required to be internalised as such?

Lacan's baby may not be a 'person' in the same way as Winnicott's, but it might require even more delicate handling. I picture Lacan's baby as an incomplete set of jigsaw pieces floating on a clear pool of water, and if successful development relies on a certain coming-together of the pieces, there will always be gaps and therefore no discernible central image. It can sometimes be difficult to locate the *I* in Lacan.

I've lingered on this because there will be times during my life when I will be convinced that the jigsaw pieces have spread so far apart they will never again come together, and if I am anything at all, it is the depthless water below. I had my first sense of the precariousness of the self when being taught French at school. I couldn't understand why the first-person singular pronoun wasn't always capitalised. I felt a falling-away in my gut, the self in peril. I was also shocked that it was two letters and not one, not a simple strike of the pen to denote an irreducible selfhood. So I do wonder to what degree our sense of self, our sensibilities, are determined by the sound and mark of our language's first-person pronoun. In English it's a single stroke and its homophones (eye/aye) a seeing-out into the world and an affirmation. The German *ich* is brittle: you can hear how it will smash. The French *je* has give: you can feel its softness. In Italian, *io* – both letters pronounced – has playfulness, a fun loss of balance. I am definitely an *ich*.

Uniform

The new house has a large garden. The garden is important, because my father wants to keep ducks. Along with cricket, they are his special interest. Because of his shift work my mother has to look after them, feed them, round them up in the evening, arms wide, body low, shooing them into their pens. When it comes to cricket, my mother learns that wives and girlfriends are expected to do the 'teas', to prepare the food, serve it to their men between innings, then clear up.

These two elements will dominate all our lives, oftentimes to the exclusion of all else. Each house move will be to increase the outside space for more ducks; the few times we go on holiday, we visit bird sanctuaries. The summers are taken up by home and away cricket matches: midweek, often twice at weekends.

But this is not how I see my father, in casual clothes outside with the ducks, building pens, filling feeding trays, or in his cricket whites, invariably as captain, moving his teammates around the field or striding out to bat, although I have these memories if I think hard enough. No: I see my father in uniform, entering the kitchen from the back door, a tall man, a lean body made compact by the stiff fabric and the tight belt of his tunic. I see him take off his helmet and hang it up, a large hand run through his thinning dark hair. Then his truncheon is removed from a special deep pocket and hung up next to his helmet. There are silver-plated numbers on his epaulettes and clipped to his lapel is the handset of his police radio. There is always the crackle of voices, glitchy, information from distant male voices I can't follow. When he presses a button on the handset, he tilts his head, cheek to lapel, and says, 'Papa Romeo 380, are you receiving me?' This is a version of him I see from the kitchen table. Not a father, or duck lover, or cricketer. A policeman.

My father's height is measured annually by the police force. He is six foot two and a half inches, he says. Over the years I never heard him round up. He remained taller than me until he died. I am six foot. Except that I'm not. I'm rounding up. Less than half a centimetre, but still.

Women who married just before the sexual revolution, weary of their husbands, encountering my father on his beat, found themselves entranced, and as he confessed in later life, propositioned him there and then on the street. According to my mother, at parties wives of other men lined up to dance with him and whispered similar things. Being with a man other women coveted was important to my mother; it's why she wanted to create a kind of mystique around him – that he was special beyond his attractiveness, like a movie star. I remember there was a rumour that a woman thought of as a bohemian type (diaphanous clothes, unruly hair) killed herself because of my father. She cleaned her house, left a note, and then threw herself under a train.

When my father is on a day shift, my mother leaves the house in the afternoon and walks to meet him on his way home. Just to be with him *sooner*, she said. Anyone who's been in love recognises this feeling. Also, she had nothing else to do after spending all morning cleaning the house, and the early afternoon pressing his shirts.

In the evening they watch television or listen to music. My father has trouble with current musical trends: he finds the Beatles' sound too bright, Bob Dylan's voice too untuneful, the Rolling Stones' manner too brash. He likes an easy melody, lyrics of love, a sweep of emotion.

At Christmas time, my mother thinks she'll be able to see Toni. Nothing has been said otherwise. On a telephone call her own mother tells her she is not welcome; she has made her bed, she is told. My mother won't see her eldest daughter again for another fourteen years.

New Possibilities

Working back from my birthday, I must have been conceived in late December 1964. My parents have been in their new home only a couple of months; they have known each other just over a year. My mother discovers she is pregnant by the end of January. She counts out the coming months on her fingers.

She prays for a boy. Prays for a boy, she later tells me, to 'make up for' the son my father lost. It may also be the case that my mother wanted a son for herself because she didn't want to feel as if she had directly replaced her daughter, but she never said this: it was always about what my father had lost and what she might give him back. I cannot think into my father at this point, how he must have felt at the prospect of a new baby only fifteen months after The Accident. My mother claims he was happy; they painted the spare room together, collected from the garage a cot, a pram, baby clothes for a boy, all used.

What is their life like now? My father is still on shift work, doubles and nights. There are ducks in the garden. In late spring the cricket season will begin. But at the same time there are letters about divorce, matters of custody that must be answered. Each week my father gives my mother housekeeping money, coins and notes which she keeps in her purse in a drawer, taking out what she needs when she needs it. The old parade of shops, a butcher, a greengrocer, a laundrette, a hairdresser, is a two-mile walk. The money runs out before the end of the week and she has to buy food on tick. It is an embarrassment, but she thinks nothing of my father buying more ducks, a new cricket bat, an LP once a week. She must make do with what she is given. My father has said that Dorothy wasn't a good housewife although she tried her best. My mother learns by trial and error what is required to be a good housewife – he doesn't think it needs explaining; his silence is enough. In his house, a kind of telepathy is required, a skill that must be learned.

My mother keeps cigarettes at the back of a kitchen drawer. She only smokes a couple a day, sitting outside in the garden, her arms resting on the bump. My father doesn't know she still smokes; last time he asked her about it, she promised that she'd given up. She daydreams of going to see Toni, if only she could get to Surbiton and back between the time my father leaves home and when she walks up the hill to meet him. She has asked my father to take her there, but he thinks it's better for everyone that she doesn't go. Every other weekend he plays cricket for a team close to his old station, a few streets away from where Toni lives, but my mother must prepare, serve and clear away the teas. She watches other children running around the clubhouse, most the same age as Toni, the age of Michael when he died, the age he would have been now.

They attend social events with policemen from the new station and their wives. My father forbids my mother to talk about the past; they are a young couple with a first child on the way. No one thinks to ask questions, suspect anything: my mother is still in her mid-twenties, my father just thirty.

Towards the end of my mother's pregnancy she gets heavier, becomes slower in her chores. My father shows his impatience. For long stretches of time he is silent, with flashes of impatience. If it wasn't for his bearing, his manner, he'd look like a sulker, a child not getting his own way, but his bearing and manner count for something: to be in his company is to be in the presence of a strong force. The combination of his height, deep voice, expressive hands, produces an expectation that he is to be attended to. And in some this provokes a willingness to serve him.

My mother remembers being told that if the bump is small, low, spread around the hips it is a girl; if it is rounder, higher, forward-facing it is a boy. She thinks that her shape this time is different to when she was pregnant with Toni. She tells my father this. She wants him to be pleased this is the case.

During the early summer months they spend time together in the garden, my mother on her knees, creating flower beds, my father mowing the lawn, moving duck pens around. On the patio a small transistor radio plays pop music. Hanging on the washing line are my father's police shirts and cricket whites. My mother knows to bring in laundry off the line before dusk, otherwise it will become damp and have to be aired, which means hanging it out again the following morning. In the hallway there is a long brown leather bag, always open. It is like a split in a large organ, a giant liver. My father's cricket bag. It smells of sweat and linseed oil. My mother has nothing of her own except clothes she now doesn't fit into. The sewing box she uses to let them out is Dorothy's.

My mother's first contraction starts on a Sunday, at a cricket match, a home match at my father's old club, not far from her parents', although that is of no use. She is looked after by the other wives and mothers. When they are the fielding side, as captain my father sends himself down to the boundary to check on her. No one expects anything to happen for a day or two; it is a week until her due date. She sits on a deckchair, squirming when the contractions come. They leave for home directly after the match, where my father rings the midwife. She will come first thing in the morning if she doesn't hear from them in the meantime.

It is 28 August 1965. The radio is on all night, tuned to light music. There is no news of great importance from around the world.

Part Two

1–10 Years Old

Birth Day

I am born late afternoon on a Sunday, the midwife present. I emerge with a dark and silver viscous sheen, which becomes thick, dark, straight hair over a round head. The rest of me is shiny pink and rose-blotched flesh. Only when I've fully flopped out into the guiding hands of the midwife does she declare: 'It's a boy!'

I am born into light and warmth and the psychical vibrations of my mother's exhausted relief, her exhausted joy. I have been prayed for, and now I am here. We must now wait for my father. It is two hours until the end of his shift.

When at last my father enters the bright room from the dark hallway, for a moment he cannot see us – the room is just a yellow, fizzing haze. Slowly his eyes adjust. My mother, dozing, stirs. There is an empty teacup on the bedside table. I am in the cot pulled alongside the bed, swaddled and quiet. He stands there in his uniform, the top button of his tunic undone, his helmet and truncheon left on the table in the hallway. His armpits are sweaty, his collar damp. He crosses over to the cot and looks down at me.

Donald Winnicott wrote that 'each baby is from the start a person and needs to be known by someone'. If that is true, then this moment matters. I am, after all, a second child for them both. For my mother I am different from her first: a boy. But for my father I can only be second.

Birth has been described as being thrown into a world not of our choosing. In his novel *The Runaway Soul* Harold Brodkey calls it 'this sort of uncancellable beginning'. Modern biology frames it not as entry but as exposure to a set affordances: 'what the environment offers the animal – what it provides or furnishes, for good or ill.' In chaos theory we learn about our 'sensitive dependence on initial conditions', more commonly known as the butterfly effect. Taken together, this means that when and where we are born, and to whom, matters to the *n*th degree.

After my mother dies, I learn via my father's third wife that my mother worried about my black hair. Michael had fair, reddish hair, as my father had as a child, and she realised – in that moment at least – that she did want me to replace Michael, to be the same. But that wasn't enough. She also wanted me to be different – better. Because she hoped it would raise her up. In that sense she is waiting for his judgement, and until that time the world in which we exist is unstable.

There is a photo I like to think was taken a few minutes later. My father is in his uniform, holding me in the air, looking directly at me, hanging there above him. As a plump baby in soft warm clothes, I am good to hold, and I sense his pleasure in the photo. There is a kind of tension in his jaw, the kind that comes when satisfaction is muscular, somatic. When I look at that photo, I like to think his grip transferred something to me that endured. That to him I was simply myself. A son to a father. Thrown into the world, yes – but caught.

Autumn

So what does my father make of me? Though I am plump and cuddlesome, I don't smile much and am not easily entertained. I don't give back and he doesn't like that; he wants chuckles when he tickles me, whereas I am fidgety, unsettled. Happier when put down, which feels like a rejection to him. According to my mother many years later, he declares that I am going to be moody and therefore unhappy in life. She starts to worry. We are now a version of what my father had before The Accident, and she is anxious about how we compare. What she doesn't realise is that Dorothy and Michael have been perfected by their early deaths, so if we are in a competition, we've already lost.

At times my mother panics. My father's mood – at home, in the garden, in the car, around others – relies on not being irritated by the world around him. She senses a kind of butterfly effect: outcomes are based on tiny sensitivities, and that involves any noise or clutter he experiences when he walks in the door. My mother fears that if the tiniest thing isn't right she'll be blamed and things will fall apart. In the end, looking after me and managing the world around my father is too much for her. She chooses the latter, because eventually I will have to do the same.

I wonder when I was named, before or after I was born. My name, at least when spoken, is a verb. To kneel. To genuflect. Its mood is imperative, a command. It was my father who chose it. Even now, after fifty-plus years, I sometimes wonder: *Is that really my name?*

My father grew up being called Mick, a name he disliked and didn't think suited him. While not quite a working-class diminutive, it lacks authority, command, stability maybe. When he left home he introduced himself as Mike, a no-nonsense name. As we know, his first son was named after him and had fair, reddish hair like my father's when he was a child. Michael also had a long face like my father, like my sister's son (also named Michael), and like my son, whose name, Macleod, shares five of the same letters. I should also confess to having Michael as a middle name. My stepsister named her son Frederick: my father's middle name.

We're a few weeks in, maybe a month, perhaps a little more. I am in my cot and my parents are in the next room watching television. It is early evening and I am crying. My father tells my mother to turn up the sound on the television. My cry is loud and persists, and the increased volume doesn't cover it. Nothing can: it's in the nature of a baby's cry to cut through everything else. My mother wants to go to me. She asks him, but my father refuses. I won't learn otherwise, he says. I cry all evening. They sit there, the sound of the television all the way up.

My parents go to bed. My crying disturbs my father, who is trying to sleep. He sends my mother to me. She can stay all night, he says.

For Lacan, the crying baby gives us a glimpse of the Real: crying as an expression of bodily need, unmediated by language – something that remains with us our whole life. A lack.

There is a less pessimistic way of looking at crying. That we are fundamentally object-seeking, our need for the 'pleasure' of connecting with another. Winnicott adds the notion of 'excitement', with its sense of precariousness – we feel most alive when on the edge of danger. Perhaps a crying baby senses what's at stake and in making a noise is choosing life.

To give Lacan his due, he also saw in a baby's cry the beginning of desire, and who'd want to live without desire?

My father is out most of the time: working long hours or playing sport. When he is home, if he isn't with his ducks, he is watching TV or sleeping. At what point, I wonder, did he realise he was having difficulty loving me? From things my mother said, it was fairly early on. It wouldn't have been unusual. A friend who attended a support group for bereaved parents once heard a mother declare the baby on her lap 'the wrong baby'.

Leonard Shengold, who specialised in the study of child abuse, coined the term 'loving hate'. I think we can intuit what this means. Most of us will have felt it, certainly towards family members, lovers or partners, and sometimes deservedly so. But when it comes to a baby there can be no 'deservedly so'. Yet it might be that this was the only emotion available to my father because I was living proof of Michael's death.

There must have been times for both my parents when I was out of focus, their vision disturbed by the semi-opaque faces that should be present before them. They'd look down at me and see others. Just for an instant. Nothing a shake of the head wouldn't dispel. But it is in these moments that my parents are reminded of what they have lost, and by extension, what needed to have happened for me to exist. My existence has come at such a price.

Mirror Phase I

We are in the garden. My father is lying on his back, holding me in the air. He holds me high, drops me down, holds me high, drops me down. It is a game, and I am laughing, laughing. I am then lying on my back and my father is on all fours over me, a looming face. He nuzzles my neck and tummy. I chortle. My mother is in the kitchen, cooking or washing up, and looks out of the window. Life is how it should be; how it has been imagined and expected, prayed for. We are all happy.

Except that's not right. Only my father is truly happy. There is a qualitative difference between his state and ours. We are happy too, but we are also thinking ahead to what might go wrong, what might displease him. Our stomachs are a little tense. This is the way it must be. To be happy, my mother whispers, we must make him happy, and to make him happy we must think our way into him and take this knowledge into ourselves and then we'll always know how to behave. Except she never has to say this; it is what psychoanalyst Christopher Bollas called the 'unthought known'.

The holding of a baby with ordinary loving care. The holding environment. The environment is a person. The environment is loving care. This is all Winnicott and being played out in a back garden. But Winnicott also said, 'The unconscious is where deprivations are kept'. And this is also what is happening here. It doesn't matter that he is large and I am small; I must make space for him and everything he is, his needs, demands, desires. And what is barely filled – me – needs to be emptied to make way for him. And as I do this, a vacuum is created and he rushes in.

I am in my mother's arms as she walks around the house, my head lolling on her shoulder, my back being tapped for any last burps. Perhaps she is singing to me, to herself, something from the radio earlier this morning when my father was shaving: 'These Boots are Made for Walkin''. We move on light feet from the bedroom into the hallway into the lounge to the French windows. There she stands on the threshold, rocking. It is autumn. There are leaves on the grass. 'It's getting colder,' she says. She turns and walks back around the house. There is a mirror in the hallway. If she stops and looks at herself she knows what she will see: she's lost too much weight and it doesn't suit her face, and her hair is a mess. My father has been on earlies this week and this means getting up at 5.30 a.m to make his breakfast. She is exhausted.

I burp.

'Good boy.'

My mother shuffles me around so I face the mirror. Chubby legs hang either side of the crook of her arm, turned inwards to support me, hand splayed across my chest to keep me steady. I am a ventriloquist's dummy. The audience I am presented to is our reflection. My mother smiles at us both and introduces me.

Except that's not right. Rather than say, 'This is Neil,' she says, 'Who's this?'

We have reached Lacan's 'mirror phase'.

At first it's a guessing game. I am being asked 'Who is this?' in the mirror. The answer cannot be 'me', because I am reaching out my hand to this *this*. My mother asks again, adding a little colour, 'Who's this handsome boy?' I am still straining forward, a chubby hand all grabby at the image. The baby in the mirror seems to be a whole thing, like a real person, whereas I can't walk, can't hold much, can't scratch an itch on one part of my body with another. But there is more. I am not interested in identification but connection. I want to touch. My mother supplies the answer: 'Yes, it's Neil, isn't it?' I turn to her. After all, I've heard my name. Maybe my chubby hands now start to grab at her. But the game is not over. My mother wants me to see myself, to get that it's me in the mirror, and as a corollary see us, mother and son, and get that too. And so she remains focused on the mirror, addressing me as the baby in the mirror and saying, 'Look, it's Neil, yes it is,' and in that moment the mirror baby becomes the real baby.

What is happening? Two things. My fidgety, uncoordinated limbs become part of me – I am a unity. But I am also split into subject and object; there is a spectral self beyond the embodied self, one that cannot be found where I am not. Perhaps it is this moment that leads to the formation of the self we address in our thoughts, the ghost in the machine. But who is talking to who? There is opportunity for confusion, for slippage, for the spectral self to become the controlling presence when there isn't anything there.

The Summer of Love

I'm under a coffee table, crawling on my hands and knees, my mother ironing. There is a song on the radio, the Phil Spector sound, full and echoey, the women's voices in rough unison as if they are singing into the same mic, vying for position, dominance, giving the performance both a big blur and a scratchy edge.

I am approaching the age at which Michael died and Toni was left with her father. If all goes well, at this point there will be a space opening out in which I will exist free of comparison, where finally difference might begin. There is also now another baby in the house – my sister, Sarah.

My mother decides she wants to be known as Maggie. My father doesn't like this; it seems frivolous, wayward, modish. He refuses to use it or allow others to do so, intervening straightforwardly: 'Her name is Margaret.' Let's remember that when he left home he chose to be Mike and not Mick.

What impression does this give of him? Of his certainty, his confidence in the world? Few people know their own mind in such a way. When you meet someone like this, it's easy to find yourself following them, even if it's just in conversation, nodding along. But it's dangerous to believe in people in such a way.

No one calls her Maggie in his presence.

———

I am a toddler and there are times when I want what I want. I writhe on the floor. If the impulse to have the world my way is too strong and my father is on his way home, my mother pleads with me: I must – must – do as she says, for all our sakes. If that doesn't work, she begs. Pure and simple: please, please. I obey, eventually. I feel my mother's relief inside us both: she doesn't trust that the world will survive if my father is disturbed. I must do my bit, which means I must participate in the world according to my mother's instruction. But I've been learning this lesson my whole short life. My mother says to me: 'If only you could smile more. Just for your dad. Please, just for me.'

I want to please him, I do. It's all I want. There are two technical ways to describe how this is done. From psychoanalysis it is cathexis, the concentration of mental energy on someone or thing, especially to an unhealthy degree. From philosophy it is intentionality. For example an idea of something, a thought about something, a feeling for something and even perhaps being in love with someone. But not, it should be noted, being loved by someone. There is nothing one can do about that.

Whatever we want to call it, this desire to please is directional: energy and focus aimed at something. Put simply: creating a centre of attention.

I am not interested in ducks. Whatever peculiar interest they hold for my father, they do not hold for me and never will. I am sort of interested in cricket, wafting a bat at a ball with all the grace of my age, never making contact. My father wants to coach me, impart knowledge, and tries not to show his impatience, but he's irritable if my mind drifts, if I don't seem to be trying. What I really like to do is dress up as a cowboy, go to the end of the garden and lay on my front playing with toy soldiers in the dirt. I like to get up close, my eyes to the ground, so the perspective seems real. From that time onwards I'm always in some kind of costume, and I'm not sure I've ever had real perspective in anything.

My mother is kneeling before me, one hand on my shoulder to keep me there, and with the index finger of her other hand she points at my temple. 'There is something evil in there,' she says, 'a nasty horrible worm.' Sometimes she says it is the Devil, the residual Calvinist in her believing that bad behaviour comes from the dark beyond.

It is around adolescence when my father starts to tell my mother that there is something broken about me, unfixable, a character flaw.

Winnicott says that to discover our deepest nature someone fundamental to us must be defied; we must be able to turn away from this person, risk losing them because of who we are, be happy to find ourselves alone. This is our true self. The next stage is to be able to set our deepest nature aside, to develop a personality for a world in which we are required to be compliant with others. To develop a false self. The language is misleading, because a good false self knows how to get along with the world but knows its deepest nature when alone.

What then of a bad false self? If sufficient emotional care isn't provided by the parent so that the child can't be happily alone, the child has to take on this role themselves to pretend the care is there. The bad false self is this pretence, and its compliance is a fear of further rejection. Fear of rejection may also present, paradoxically, as the opposite to compliant – a contrarian. Or sometimes both: an almost unbearable oscillation between both states. But in the end a bad false self skews everything, all relationships are precarious, and worst of all, we never see people for who they are because we can't see them straight. A child with a bad false self wants to be comfortable, willingly compliant, but it's impossible because they don't know what they want or what others might be willing to offer them. And this gets worse in adulthood. It's fucking exhausting, believe me.

The Wider World

My mother and I, with my sister in a pushchair, have come to the gardens of Hayes Library. There are pale pink and yellow rose bushes in the centre of trimmed lawns. Opposite the library, over the main road, is a red-brick church hall with large blue doors. We are walking around the library gardens because my mother is telling me: 'This morning you are going in.' If I don't do what she says, she will tell my father. This time she will tell my father. This time has been every time, but this time never comes.

Outside the church hall, other mothers are saying goodbye to their children. As she has done every day, my mother points to the other boys. Don't I want to be like them? I tell her I don't want to go; I don't want to play with other children; I don't care that big boys go to nursery. I say I want to stay with her. I want to go home. I want my cowboy outfit and my soldiers. I cry. My sister is crying. I am promised sweets. Then, as she has done every day, she asks the mothers of other boys if their sons will take me in, look after me when I'm in there. I stand behind her, clutching her leg. But on this day a little girl appears. I've seen her before. She lives in a house up the road. I don't know her name, but I point and want to know: is *she* going in? My mother sends pleading signals to the little girl's mother.

'Anna is going in,' the girl's mother says. 'She will look after you.'

I come out from behind my own mother's leg. Anna offers me her hand and leads me up the steps and in through the blue doors.

One afternoon, walking back through the library gardens, my mother tells me and my sister about a conversation she was having with the other mothers at the nursery doors. Who would they save first if their husbands and children were drowning? She was surprised, she says, to hear that all the other women would choose their children. She tells us she would save our father. Our father is special, in ways other fathers are not. We know this, but she is saying more than that. There is new information. Our safety is conditional; our lives are now precarious, based on whether our father is in peril at the same time. Did something shift in me that day? I can't be sure, but I do know that I remember my mother's words clearly.

Later on I will realise that this is how my mother was able to leave Toni – she chose to save my father.

It is 1974. I am at primary school. There are two Deborahs, a Susan and a Cathy. I can't seem to get them out of my mind. It is assembly. While I sit cross-legged on the hall floor, Cathy, in the choir, is seated on the stage. I can stare at her at much as I like. And I do.

The choir sings 'Morning Has Broken'. The sunlight from the high windows becomes a glistening mist, drifting through the exposed rafters and settling on the choir. I decide that Cathy is an angel. I am in a kind of swoon – no latency period for me.

A few weeks before Christmas, we construct a big red postbox out of cardboard and crêpe paper, into which we'll post the cards we've made for classmates, and on the last day of the term it will be opened and our cards will fall spillingly out. I make cards for the two Deborahs, Susan and Cathy. I write *I love you* in each. From my mother's jewellery box I steal four rings and place one in each envelope.

What did I want? To marry them all? Maybe it was simply the desire for an inner state that I thought I saw on their faces, especially Cathy singing in the choir in the sunlight.

The morning the postbox is opened and the letters are handed out, I feel like I am in a dream where I've come to school with no clothes.

Desire is a deprivation in the unconscious. This is Lacan, mixed with Winnicott.

A new family moves in next door: there are four children, all older than me. They're noisy and argumentative. We often hear shouting through the walls. At least once a week the younger of the two daughters storms out the house, down the garden path, and when on the street turns and faces the house and carries on shouting.

My mother explains that we are a different kind of family, that our dad doesn't like noise and fuss. I don't need to be told this. For as long as I can remember we've been given a warning: 'Your father is on his way home.' It is in this way that my father looms large even in his absence; we have to be good for a man who isn't visible to us. This is how you create a god. I remember he loomed largest in those moments when he was about to appear. After all, who doesn't fear an angry god walking into the room?

There are days when he is in the house and we make noise and we hear him shout, 'Stop that noise.' At which point we fear, as my mother fears, that we have ruined the rest of the day. Is it ruined? Yes, for us, because we now fear his mood: we whisper, walk softly, open and close doors with the delicacy of thieves. But the day is not ruined for my father, because it is now quiet and will remain so.

Our home is not always like this. My best friend, Thomas, has restricted growth. He lives at the bottom of the street, in a home very different from ours. Thomas's parents, Josie and Derek, are antique dealers. They are gentle and softly spoken. Derek is always in soft, oversized clothes, jumpers and cords; Josie has a kind of scruffy glamour, a kind of swish as she walks into the room. She has a confidence my mother worries will irritate my father, and I hear her say 'Oh, that Josie Wood' whenever they've all met somewhere.

My father calls Thomas 'Champ'. He carries Thomas under his arm and claims not to know where he is, turning on the spot, a hand spanned across his eyes, looking out as if Thomas is lost at sea. Thomas thinks it's funny. I think it's funny. We both laugh.

If Thomas stays for tea, my father might eat with us, around the kitchen table, or sometimes he eats in the lounge, where my mother will take in his food on a tray. When it's time for him to leave, Thomas will take it upon himself to go straight into the lounge to say goodbye to my father. This makes me nervous; we don't disturb my father when he's eating and watching television. But Thomas goes in and my father looks over and says, 'Hi there, Champ. What you doing? You off? Come here,' and he does something – pulls a face, makes a burping sound – to make Thomas laugh. I stand in the doorway. I am told to either come in or leave but to stop hovering. I think Thomas is lucky to receive such attention from my father. It excites me to witness it.

My mother used to tell a story of being at a party on Christmas Eve with my father. She is at the buffet table putting a plate of food together for him while he stands next to her indicating what he wants. A neighbour standing nearby says to my father, 'It's not love, it's fear.' My parents immediately leave, and my father threatens to cancel Christmas if she doesn't go to the neighbour's house and explain.

Two things stand out. First, that my father couldn't leave anything hanging – he had to set the record straight – and secondly, my mother's respect for the man who'd said those words. Even at the time she liked someone who could see through my father. Which means that she knew the truth about him.

My mother comes into my bedroom. It's early evening in winter. She turns off my bedroom light and tells me to get onto the floor. 'We're pretending we're not here,' she says.

'That your dad is not here.'

Outside, a woman is shouting 'I know you're in there.' She knows he's in there because she knows his shifts. It is a woman we once visited. She had lots of dogs.

After ten minutes, there are flashing lights on the ceiling. I look out of the window. The woman is escorted from our front garden to the police car. She claims that my father promised to marry her and now he is going back on it. She wasn't the only semi-stranger to become fixated on my father. It's extraordinary what being tall, dark and handsome could achieve in the 1970s.

After school, my friend Peter is coming to tea. We argue about which of the different routes to my house is the quickest, and decide to each go the way he thinks is best. We promise to walk. After all, it is the route that is being tested, not how fast we can run.

When I arrive home Peter is there, and so is my father. He demands to know where I've been all this time. I look at Peter and say, 'He ran.'

Peter is immediately sent home and I'm told to fetch ... *the cane*. I didn't even know we had a cane! I am directed to it. Has this punishment been prepared for? It seems so.

The cane is the length of a magician's wand. There is almost no give in it. 'What did I do wrong?' I ask.

'You answered back.'

My father tells me to hold out my hand. I do so, slowly unpeeling my fingers from my palm. Five thwacks. I can't close my hand for days. I am never caned again. It's like it never happened.

For balance:

Each summer my father takes me to cricket matches to see Kent play in Canterbury, but there is always at least one day at a Test match at Lord's or The Oval. In these days you could still sit on the grass by the boundary rope and throw the ball back to the fielders after it had gone for four. We eat packed lunches made by my mother. In the afternoon, my father dozes off. No impatience or irritability – after all, the sun is out and we are at the cricket.

Every Wednesday evening, my father teaches table tennis at a youth centre for boys who have been in trouble. Policemen, ex-policemen, prison officers, ex-prison officers work there as coaches and mentors. My father is very good at this, often persuading boys to attend in the first place, even going to their homes to collect them when they don't show up. He believes, as he often says, that these boys are just going through a 'stage' and will settle down when they find a steady girlfriend. He believes in the power of women to steady a man.

As part of his beat, he visits those who live alone and need company. He is patient and chatty. He puts in the effort. He is generous with time and money, with the things he has. He is good to his friends, sought out and trusted for sound advice. Many of his friends rely on him throughout their lives. When he dies, the church is full.

Let me be clear: people weren't duped by him; it was the right response to his actions and behaviour. And he wasn't pretending. It wasn't done out of a sense of duty. A lot of people loved and respected him because out in the world he was a kind and generous man.

Some mornings, if his shift doesn't start until late, he sits at the kitchen table and sings along to music on the radio. He has a good voice, tuneful, rich, without the need for flourish or affectation to express emotion. He mimes playing the piano on the tabletop even if there is no piano in the music. If he's being watched he acts as if he's a puppet at this piano, happy to be seen as a joker. He still likes sentimental, melodic music, songs about love rather than heartbreak.

Early Sunday evenings, in winter, he plays music, sitting cross-legged in front of the record cabinet, its concertina doors open. He selects an album, tips it out by its top corner, removes the LP in its white inside sleeve and slides it out. He then flips it round so he can hold it by its rim in his palms, fingers splayed and taut, and glance at the label for a second. He then leans up to place it on the deck, and carefully drops the needle on the dark band at the outer edge. The initial crackle is a sound I still miss. He then sings along and mimes the strumming of a guitar. I watch this through a half-opened door. Sometimes my mum joins him, perched on the arm of the sofa. Tonight he is playing his favourite song on Crosby, Stills, Nash & Young's *Déjà Vu*, Graham Nash's 'Our House'. He plays it over and over.

Wish fulfilment or deep irony? Neither. It's just a lovely melody.

One night, when I am ten years old, my mother wakes me and takes me downstairs to the lounge. The concertina doors of the record cabinet are open, LP covers spread across the floor. She tells me to sit where my father usually sits, but to shuffle along a little so she can sit next to me. She wants to play me records because, she says, my father is worried I don't like music. I am unaware I don't like music, but I understand what she means: I do not behave like my father when he listens to music. She plays me Crosby, Stills, Nash & Young, Simon & Garfunkel, Cat Stevens, Richie Havens.

When Richie Havens played the Fairfield Halls, Croydon, she tells me, she and my father went with friends, a couple I know to be tall and smartly dressed accountants (whatever those are). Everyone else was a hippy: long hair, kaftans, Afghan coats, beads. 'Your dad was the first up and dancing. We all were, as a group, because of your dad.'

I am then told another story.

When I was four years old, my father produced and directed a Metropolitan Police charity event, a sketch show involving, among other things, policemen wearing tutus with helmets and boots, swinging truncheons and dancing rudimentary ballet steps to Tchaikovsky's 'Dance of the Cygnets' from *Swan Lake*. My mother goes to a cabinet and shows me a copy of the local newspaper. The headline is about the first moon landing, but the front-page photo is of my father dressed as Shirley Bassey, singing 'Big Spender'. My mother stands up and acts it out for me, demonstrating to me how a man might exaggerate his movements to be a woman. She then tells me how angry she was when she was only picked as a backing dancer, but she 'showed them', at which point I am witness to some hip swivels and high kicks. I can see how aggrieved she was, and how right she felt in proving them wrong. 'Your father put his whole life into that show, and when it finished he slept for two days straight.'

We hear my father come in. My mother doesn't panic or hurry me to bed. When he walks into the lounge she says, 'We were just playing some records.' 'I hope you're looking after them,' he says, but not irritably. He looks down at the covers out on the floor and spots Richie Havens's live double album. 'Did you listen to "Freedom"?' he asks. 'Yes,' I say. 'Great track,' he says. 'But now time for bed.' My mother guides me away. From the doorway, I watch as he folds his big body down onto the floor, crossing his legs in front of the record cabinet. He holds up the cover of *Déjà Vu*. 'Did you play him "Our House"?' he asks my mother. 'I did,' she says. 'Did you like it?' he asks me. 'I did, Dad,' I say. 'I thought it was a great track.'

I can remember times from my childhood, certain scenes, discrete and closed off, mainly my mother's determination to manage my father's needs as a constant. But I don't remember what I was like, as it were: what it felt like to be me. I certainly didn't stand out, in lucky possession of abilities of note. I was a little more striking-looking than some other children: my hair was black, my eyes blue, and dinner ladies commented on and coveted my long eyelashes. I had friends, although I preferred to be with girls.

What would I have said about my feelings for my parents? That I loved my mother? Yes, I would have said so. That I feared my father, his moods, his temper? Definitely. But I would also have said that I found other fathers strangely wanting, as if they weren't present enough, solid enough, not quite in possession of sufficient gravitational pull for the world to coalesce around them, to give the world its structure. Every time a friend came around and my father was there I felt immense pride, and a belief that they would see the world differently, see *me* differently, by being in range of his force field.

Part Three

11–15 Years Old

The Country

We move house. From the suburbs into the country, to the border of Kent and East Sussex, to a small cottage in a valley with two streams that cross at the bottom of the garden. There are three acres of old apple orchard and woodland. Over the lane is a path to a newly built reservoir. The nearest house is half a mile away, the closest village, by the quickest route, a mile and a half. This is a new world. The walk to the school bus takes thirty minutes along narrow verges of rutted fields, then it's another twenty minutes on the bus to school. We have moved here so my father can breed and sell ducks with a view to doing this full-time after he retires from the police force after twenty-five years' service, at forty-eight, only a few years away.

For the second time, my mother has had to leave her job and all her friends. The new house is an hour by bus from the nearest train station and most of her friends do not have cars. No one visits her. Because my father doesn't want to transfer out of the Metropolitan Police, he stays with the noisy neighbours three nights a week, coming home on Tuesday evenings and on Friday for the weekend. This is new for us – days without my father – and the house changes: there is more talk, more arguments and in the evening choosing what is on the TV feels like a liberation we can't quite believe. But it also means my mother does most of the work at the new house. Tussocky and sodden, the ground makes it difficult to build secure duck pens. No matter what is done, foxes find their way in and kill the ducks. This, says my father, is her fault. The cottage has low ceilings with exposed beams and my father keeps hitting his head. He blames my mother for rushing him into buying it. Despite all the physical work, she puts on weight.

I am not unhappy. The house is cosy; there is much to explore in the woods. My new school is small and without a sixth form. It has a uniform, but ties aren't required. There are four Catherines in my class, two of whom I find very pretty, and in another class there is Beverley, who I can't believe can be so beautiful. I've never seen anyone like her before. She seems to have come from off the TV.

Leaving for school one morning, I peer at myself in the mirror by the front door. My mother appears behind me. She looks into the mirror and declares me handsome. Not a handsome boy. Just: handsome. I hear something in her voice, as if this pronouncement is something that is really the case, something I should take for granted because she knows it to be true. I have never thought of myself in these terms, despite my interest in girls and their occasional interest in me.

It makes sense that my mother decides this for me. Since I was born she has managed who/what I am on behalf of my father, and because she has made us believe he is infallible, being in service to him confers on her some of his authority. This is especially the case in terms of handsomeness, a subject often spoken about in our home.

When we watch TV my mother always remarks how much actors look like him: Charlton Heston, James Garner, Clint Eastwood. They look like *him*. He is the exemplar. So my mother's declaration, standing behind me as I look in the mirror, is transformational, and from that morning I have a categorical belief in my own handsomeness. Or at least in that other person's handsomeness – the boy in the mirror who looks a lot like me.

It's a Sunday, and my father's forty-fourth birthday. We've been in the new house a few months. My mother has been working hard every day, securing the pens, clearing away overgrown rhododendrons, feeding the ducks morning and night. She misses her friends. She has no money of her own, and because of the cost of the move, what she is given for housekeeping doesn't stretch beyond essentials. All she can afford to buy him for his birthday is a pair of gardening gloves. He is displeased, and the day is spent in silence.

Two months later, it is my mother's birthday, and my father gives her a pair of gardening gloves in return. This pleases him. In many ways this is cruellest thing he will do to her; it's vindictive, nasty, an easy, cheap hit. To be cruel in this way requires the intention to hurt someone emotionally. There may be psychological consequences, but at the time it was my father's objective to hurt her in the moment. Unlike torture, cruelty also requires an emotional gain – gratification – for the perpetrator. This makes it doubly hurtful to my mother. Not only does she have to endure the cruelty, but she has to accept that my father has chosen to be cruel to her. It is another day of silence.

Above the wardrobe in my parents' bedroom there is a shotgun; a box of cartridges is in the top drawer of a dresser. I often take down the shotgun, aim it, and pull the triggers: *bam, bam*. I skulk about, imagining what it would be like to kill my father: *bam, bam*. But mostly I stay in my bedroom with a generalised sick feeling day and night.

Weeks later, during a row, I hear my father take down the shotgun and say to my mother, 'One barrel for you, one for me.' I am not being entirely honest here: my memory is, 'One barrel for you, one for him.'

During another row I hear my mother say, 'I wish you'd just drive us all off a cliff.' The silence after this stretches out. She knows what she's said. She has reminded him of his part in the death of another family. My father leaves and doesn't return for the weekend. I hope he's driven himself off a cliff. But he returns the following week, and now the days of silence need no inciting incident; they are how we live.

Split

We are at a critical juncture. I have been stuck writing about this moment more than any other. I don't know how to express the nature of the split that's about to happen, its importance. But this is when there became two of me. I don't know when I realised this was the case – days later, years later, only recently – but it happened around this time. For a while one half of me was closed off to the other. Then, a year or so later, the arrangement reversed, the earlier version of me disappearing in the rear-view mirror as though it had never existed. But we're not there yet. Right now there is the me at home – quiet, timid, fearful – and the me at school: disruptive, argumentative, never quiet. Had you asked me whether there was a difference between these two places, I wouldn't have known what you were talking about. Sometimes it requires someone else to make the truth real to us. It takes the person who legislates the world to know. And so I will only come to know about this other version of myself from my father, when he hears it from my teachers, which is what is happening right now, at parents' evening.

I can picture what is happening, sitting on the stairs at home, picking at my nails. I opted out of last period to help set out the tables and chairs in the school hall. I can see my teachers, my report card open, opposite my father. I try to imagine what they might be saying, based on what I'm like at school, but everything is vague, hazy, as if when I leave the house in the morning I change and become someone different, then on returning home I leave this other person in the fields. But as I sit on the stairs, this other self is coming into focus. It won't require him to come home and explain it to me, because I can hear him hearing it, and in this way it becomes known to me.

Time moves slowly. The lane outside the house is narrow and seldom used: whenever I hear a car my stomach drops until I hear a gear change and I know it's passing, driving up and over the hill.

I hear the slow crunch of gravel, a car engine being switched off. The garage isn't next to the house; it will take a couple of minutes for my parents to walk back down the drive, along the road and to the house. I am terrified and scramble up the stairs and into my bedroom. The front door opens and my father calls, 'Get down here!' I know not to hesitate. I pass my sister looking out of her bedroom. At the bottom of the stairs, I notice that my mother has been crying. She shakes her head at me: *What have you done?* the gesture says. My father summons me to him. He points to exactly where he wants me to stand. When I reach him, he knocks me down, a hard slap of his large hand across the side of my head. He tells me to stand up. I do so, unsteadily. He slaps me again. This time I refuse to stand up until he promises he won't hit me. He orders me back up. I do not obey. He pulls me up. I clutch at his legs. He tries to free himself, as if I am sticky weeds he has found himself caught in. In the tight space between the dinner table and the wall his large feet trample over and around me. Somehow I am pulled up, held away from him and hit again. It feels like a knockout blow. He wants me up again, but I scramble away, up the stairs. 'I'll deal with you later,' he says. He disappears into the lounge and I hear the television being turned on.

'It was the worst thing they could have said: "Too much to say for yourself. Cheeky, disruptive."'

I am in my bedroom, wiping crying-snot from my nose with the back of my hand, streaking it across my trousers. My mother gives me a hanky from my father's drawer in the kitchen. The hanky has his initials, M.G., embroidered on it in blue. She sits beside me and describes the scene. Each teacher had my school report in front of them, but the instant my father, still in his uniform, sat down, they realised I would be in more trouble than they'd expected and regretted what they'd written.

'He could see they were nervous, and that irritated him. He made them read the report out and then moved onto the next teacher, who said the same thing. And then the next. It was awful.' Then she says, 'Why? Why?'

I have no answer. It's a truth. At school I am this person.

Still she asks, 'Why?' I suppose what she wants to know is how come I've let her down after all she's done for me. In many ways this evening is a moment of truth for her: I am not perfect and never have been and now it's out there –

things can never go back to the way they were; the illusion is broken.

I have a question. I am bolder now, my other self is not so far away, not so much of a blur. And so I redirect the 'why' and ask, 'Why is he the way he is?'

It is then she tells me about my father's accident, and about her daughter. Most of what I wrote at the start of this book was laid out that evening, both in detail and generally, but what I take in is the death of this boy, and that there is a half-sister who used to live under my grandparents' flat. But my mother keeps coming back to The Accident, the terribleness of it, and what my father has had to live with since then. He blames himself, she says, for not saving them. It isn't an explanation for what happened tonight; it's an excuse for why he's been the way he is all my life. She's heard my question and answered it, but it's not what I hear.

In the morning I do not have a black eye, but the outer rim of my eye socket is grazed. I go to school and I do not change my behaviour, but I am changed. I am shaken, fearful. I don't feel safe. There is a sensation in my stomach that catches me unawares: a sickness, a dropping away, emptiness falling into emptiness – uncatchable. At night I lie in bed and think back to before I was born, to the time before The Accident, and try to see the future from that point. I imagine a swerve of the car, the two cars just missing each other, and a world without me. I cannot resist trying to feel what might have been. It's giddying. But there is something else. The terrifying sense of the possibility of my non-existence is a new kind of knowledge about the world – a previously hidden dimension is revealed. It's my first confrontation with nothingness, a true depthless other side of life. As if my own split is reflected back by a world now split: there is what is there and has always been there, but that is only half of it. On the other side there is what I can only call the abyss.

My thoughts become obsessive, and I say to myself over and over: *What if there had been no accident? What if . . . ? What if . . . ? What if . . . ?* I don't think about Michael or Toni. Or my mother or father. I am my only concern. And I do not feel safe.

When I arrive at school the next day, it seems I have been put in the remedial classes for all subjects and am on report. My form teacher shrugs and seems almost apologetic. But it has been decided. Within a week, I return myself to my regular classes and no one mentions anything. I presume my father believed that his instructions would be followed and thought no more of it. He never went to a parents' evening again.

Among photographs of me as a baby, and my parents as younger people, there are photographs of a woman and a child. I've seen them lots of times and always ask who they are, as if the answer I'm given doesn't make sense: 'Neighbours from before you were born.' The photographs are black-and-white, with a white border, a sharpish serrated edge.

Sitting on the sofa, my father safely back in London, my mother is handing them to me, as if providing proof. They would have been taken between 1962 and 1963, but Dorothy looks pre-War, wearing a fitted gabardine macintosh, sturdy buckled shoes, her hair in pin curls. In one photograph she stands with a pram outside a terraced house. The photographs of Michael are professional, a baby sitting up against an indistinct background. He is an odd-looking boy with a pronounced rectangular head, a curiously grown-up face. There are a few photos of Toni, and I remember thinking I had always thought of them as photos of my mother as a baby. The ghosts within me have now been given names, shapes, brought to life; they are no longer an unknown thought.

For the next few weeks at least, I feel full up with Michael and Toni. I am jostled by them as they make room inside me, as they grow up inside me: Michael as he might have been if he'd lived, and Toni, now fourteen and very real but somehow more difficult to imagine for that reason. It is hard to have strange new people in your head who are more imaginary than real, and whose existence or non-existence makes you who you are – or in this case, that you are at all. If I am more split at that point than before, it means that at home I am even quieter than I was before, spending hours alone thinking about them, and yet each morning as I walk over the fields to catch the school bus, my personality grows larger and larger, noisier and noisier.

On reflection, I cannot blame the split on my new knowledge, but I think it did accelerate what was already happening – Michael and Toni's presence as an absence in me compounded an emptiness I was already feeling. I think this goes to the heart of what this book is about. In some sense all my mother did was provide the reason I was becoming split, something that was going to happen then or later, with or without knowing about Michael and Toni. But I do think that being told at that time made the process irreversible and more extreme.

The Other House

'Want to be the lead singer in my band?'

This is Tom Yates. He's appeared from nowhere, into a patch of sunlight near the dining hall back door. He has a triangular head, greased and spiked hair, and big, healthy teeth. He is smiling. Over time I realise Tom always smiles – he finds the world funny.

His appearance is a surprise; he's in the year above and has never spoken to me before. For reasons I can't fathom even now, I say, 'I'd rather be a drummer.'

He laughs at this. 'You're a loudmouth … you're a lead singer.'

During assembly the following day, Tom stops by where I am sitting and says I'll need a punk name, like Sid Vicious or Johnny Rotten. I ask him if he has one. He does. 'Shit Harry,' he says.

Our first couple of rehearsals are in the school music hut, but after complaints of noise we move to Tom's house. The Yateses live in an annexe of a country manor. Tom's father, Brian, is dean of the Slade School of Fine Art; Pauline, his mother, once Brian's student, is a sculptor. During the week, Brian drives to London in a red Mini Cooper; at the weekend he is fortifying a barn against nuclear attack. Pauline seems to wear the same clothes every day: jeans and an old navy-blue jumper. Her dark hair is cut in a dead-straight bob, and between its sheer sides I'm not sure I ever see her smile. Unlike my mother, she never seems to do any housework.

We practise in a large room with walls of whitewashed brickwork, the flagstone floor worn smooth. It is a library of sorts, its open shelves crammed with large art books. We rehearse in the afternoons and late into the night. No one seems to care about the noise.

Dinner – *supper* – is cooked on an Aga and eaten around a long wood table, in the centre of which there is always a large oval plate of grilled vegetables I don't recognise: aubergine, artichoke. I have never served myself before; I usually sit at our kitchen table and am given a plate of food.

Brian collects books. There are rooms full of unopened boxes from collections he's bought at auction. At one point we build a fort from the boxes of books; fourteen-year-old boys are still children half the time. The television is in a small room upstairs, with a threadbare sofa and two hardback chairs. This is perhaps the most shocking of all the differences between the houses.

I can't ever remember feeling comfortable at the Yateses' house; I lived in a bungalow where shoes were taken off at the door, fitted carpets were hoovered into the corners twice a week, and no one was allowed food or drink in the lounge except for my father, who ate dinner on a tray in front of the television. It would be wrong to say there were no books in our house, but these were mostly biographies of sportsmen and large illustrated books about ducks. There were no novels at all, not a Dickens or a Graham Greene, or even a Len Deighton. In the Yateses' home, the history of ideas, the world of art, the potential to contribute to either, or even both, was what mattered; in my home it was good manners, clean hands, quiet.

Over the first few visits, the house is hazy; it is as if I need to squint to see it clearly, or as if too much new information is being given to me and the overload makes me dizzy. I feel strangely insubstantial when I am there. I feel like an imposter, as if Tom has made a mistake: he's brought someone home from the wrong tribe: different language, different customs. When I return home to the cleanliness, the fitted carpet, the quiet, I realise that there are alien landscapes on this earth, that certain topographical differences can be vast, categorical. If the Yateses' house is destabilising, then my house has, for once, become a comfort, or at least my bedroom has. But there is a battle going on: difference is now more appealing than comfort, and what is alien offers an escape. I am at the Yateses' every weekend.

It becomes quickly evident that I cannot sing. Only I seem to care about this. Tom says it doesn't matter as long I look angry, jump up and down and shake my fist at the audience. And if I want, I can spit. The band is called Curfew and we cover songs by The Stranglers. For the school music competition that year we perform 'Dagenham Dave' and 'Death and Night and Blood'. A girl playing a version of 'Greensleeves' on the oboe wins. It doesn't matter. After the competition it is me and Tom who are surrounded by girls.

On the bus to a sports event at another school, a girl named Kate tries to get her hand down my trousers. Then Hazel, who is *two years above*, asks me out. Going out involves standing around during break saying nothing for a couple of days. But such is my confidence that I even ask Beverley Hooper out. She says no: she's going out with Steve Prince, the best footballer at school, which I suppose is fair enough. Then there is Rachel Jones, from one year above. I receive letters from her, delivered by her friend, and I am asked to respond in kind. I do my best. At the youth club, a girl from my year says she'd like to take her clothes off for me.

My attractiveness – if you'll forgive me – derives from a mixture of three aspects: because of my mother I believe I am handsome (confidence); I am the lead singer in the only band in the school (uniqueness); and I don't seem to care what anyone thinks about me (arrogance), something I am only now learning about myself. My only rival is Tom, except he doesn't appear that interested in girls; from the age of four, this has not been something that can be said about me. So that's another thing I have. I'm willing. I'm not sure that's why Kate wanted to get her hand down my trousers. Maybe I was just her type.

If I walk across the fields as if to go to school, but instead take a left behind the pub and follow the path to a wide stream that needs jumping over with the help of overhanging branches, then make my way across a large paddock, there is a small housing estate. At the rear of one garden, Rachel Jones is waiting for me. It is here I learn the reason for the letters. Being in the year below, I am an embarrassment to her, and things must be handled discreetly. She shows me into a garden shed, where we kiss and I am allowed to pull her denim shirt free from her jeans and cup my hand over a breast. I am thirteen.

At Christmas, my father becomes very ill with shingles in his mouth. He is in bed for days, unable to speak or eat. My mother's best friend and her husband come to stay. Anne, a Catholic (this is new to me in its specificity), sits beside my father and prays for him. I know enough to realise how much my father will hate this kind of fuss.

Anne is young and pretty. She has a kind of glamour: big blonde hair, tumbling curls. She is ten years younger than my mother. To a boy at school, I say, 'Miss World has come to stay.'

It is a Sunday, and we are rehearsing at James the drummer's house. James is six foot three and lives with his mother, who is from Bermuda and the same height. She is white, but her skin is very tanned. She has an American accent, or at least long vowels, an appealing easy slur. She is an astrologist and wears a long scarf around a mass of curly hair, the ends of the scarf falling down her back. She wears long diaphanous dresses that float around her dark ankles and flat sandals on dark feet. My mother is entranced by her. So am I. Her name is Wendy.

We are standing, the band is standing, outside James's house. It is summer, warm. There is a long swing gate between us and the road, which gives onto a narrow lane. Some boys pass. They stop. There are five of them, all older than us, older than Tom. Sixteen, perhaps. They want to know what we're doing. 'Practising,' I tell them. It's too quickly said, sounds a bit pompous, as if I'm overly pleased with myself. They jeer and tease. 'Let's hear yer.' 'Gis a go of your guitar.' 'Bet yer shit.' I can't remember exactly what I say to this; it isn't anything provocative, but I'm known to be the bigmouth with a girlfriend in their year. One of the boys moves forward. He is small, stocky, with a head like a concrete slab, his features etched out. He wants me to come out onto the road and say it again. There is laughter. I refuse. He is matter-of-fact: I either come out from behind the gate and say it again, or he'll get me at school tomorrow. I choose to stay where I am. He steps further forward and points at me. 'You're going to get it,' he tells me.

At home I tell my mother and admit that I am frightened. 'Ask your dad what to do,' she says. I don't understand; she has never said anything like this before.

'I can't,' I say. She cajoles: 'Just go in there and say, "Dad, a boy is threatening to beat me up at school – what should I do?"'

I don't know what I'm most scared of: disturbing my father watching television in the lounge, or being beaten up tomorrow. Different metrics, equal intensity. But I am also a little exhilarated. I *want* to ask my father this question, because I want to hear what he says. I want my predicament, my worry, something that is happening in my world, to enter his world and be acted on *by him*. I have no doubt he possesses the answer I need. Behind the lounge door, his large face lit only by the flickering of the television, I am sure he knows what others don't: he is in possession of knowledge that will solve my problem. My mother has followed me to the door of the lounge. 'It'll be fine,' she says.

I knock and walk in. There is a big bay window to my left; the curtains are open, it is dusk outside and objects in the room are reflected in the glass. My father sits in his armchair, feet up on a footstool, the television on. I am nervous, awkward in my body; I stand off-centre in the room, hovering on the periphery of his eyeline.

'Dad,' I say. I immediately sense that he's irritated at being disturbed. I take a breath; explain things as plainly as I can. 'This boy today, a boy from school, says he's going to beat me up tomorrow, and I don't know what to do. What do you think I should do?'

My father doesn't pause to think. He doesn't look up from the television. All he says is, 'Just give him a good hiding.'

I stand there for a second or two, but I know there isn't going to be any more. How can there be? The objects in the room are ghostly reflections on the glass. I am no more substantial than my surroundings.

There are two main thoughts about free will: the hard determinist – no wiggle room – and some version where there is wiggle room. The first basically means that what we do now is *entirely* dependent on 'antecedent causes' going all the way back to the Big Bang; the second version suggests that if these 'antecedent causes' aren't sufficiently strong to lead to the next effect, there might be a space into which we can insert ourselves and freely choose.

This is what happened here. My father was watching television and didn't want to be disturbed: strong antecedent causes were pressing forward. I walked in. I was a new causal condition, but not sufficiently strong enough to interrupt what was pressing him forward – there was no gap into which I could wiggle. This is not to excuse his behaviour. It's an explanation.

The following morning, I am walking past the music hut. The boy, with two others, is in front of me. The other two boys grab me and hold me against the wall. The main boy punches me a few times in the stomach. Like gangsters roughing me up, they push me to the ground and kick me. The grass verge is muddy and my uniform is streaked with it. There is mud on my face, in my hair. It happens again at lunchtime. Again during afternoon break. And then it's over.

It is Guy Fawkes Night and I am looking through the large kitchen window. For some reason, my mother is rolling around on the front lawn with Anne. I look around to check that I am not dreaming. I turn back to the window. It's the same: outside on the front lawn, my mother is rolling about with Anne. It's then I notice my father, standing on the drive, watching, as if he's the one in a dream. There isn't the noise one might associate with this kind of scene, as if the sound has been turned down.

After a few seconds the sound is turned on. There is shouting. My mother is angry, cursing. Pointing and swearing at Anne. I don't go outside. I have other, more important worries. I am home early because what was supposed to be a great evening has gone horribly wrong. It was my band's first real gig, at a fireworks event in the grounds of a large house given over to the village for the night. We had rehearsed ten songs. By the end of the first song, rotten apples and potatoes were being thrown at me, thrown hard so they hurt and burst on impact. The boy who beat me up was there, at the front, jeering. He had a bucket next to him. He bent at the knees, hand blindly dipping into the bucket, then threw whatever he found in his hand straight at me. Others had buckets. This had been planned. By the middle of the second song my clothes were covered and I had to wipe my face clean with my T-shirt. I was the sole target. The rest of the band were only hit by the occasional ricochet or a bad throw. This wasn't just about my run-in with the boy a few months ago; this was about something else. It is cool to play the electric guitar; every boy fancies themselves a drummer; bass players are unassuming to the point of invisibility. The something was me being the lead singer. *Who the fuck are you to think you can do this?* It's so brazen, isn't it, to stand there front and centre and by the nature of what you're doing demand to be looked at and listened to? 'I want *you* to look at *me*, *you* to listen to *me*.'

By song three it was over, and I fled to my mother's car. We were home hours earlier than expected, and I went straight to my bedroom.

I am not sure what drew me back into the kitchen. Decades on, I still don't know what brought Anne to our house that night. She lived where we used to live, over an hour's drive away. It couldn't have been to inform my mother of her affair with my father, because my mother wasn't supposed to be there. It couldn't have been to snatch some private time with my father; she had a flat of her own. Maybe my father had broken off their affair and she'd followed him home? I don't know. But as I say, I had other, more important things on my mind.

The following day I am kicked out of the band and replaced by a boy from the year below. He is that year's version of Tom, angular, sinewy, his parents artists of some sort. A few weeks later in maths, James confesses that rehearsals aren't going well. Yes, Jez is a better singer than I am, but he can't remember the words. 'At least he can sing,' I say. James laughs. 'It doesn't matter if you can't remember the words.'

I remember thinking: being able to sing is a talent; remembering the words is an ability. I hated myself for only possessing the latter. Also, I suspect that had they ever played a gig, Jez wouldn't have been pelted with rotten food. Attracting that kind of attention is a talent.

I am not my father's son. No one would have dared throw rotten food at him. Plus, he had a really good singing voice. And he was able to remember the words to 'Big Spender'.

Six years later, I am working part-time in a music shop. I am at the far end, among the drums, tidying up the cymbals and cymbal stands. The shop bell rings. I turn around and it is him, the boy who beat me up and pelted me with vegetables. He's unchanged: short, stocky, all muscle. He walks up to me. I sense he is nervous and feels out of place. His body twitches as he sorts himself out, settles his shoulders. He has something to say, he says. He wants to apologise for what he did to me. And he says it, 'Sorry,' then stays where he is, obviously not sure what should happen next. I say something like, 'That's fine, of course that's fine. Thank you.'

I still remember the extraordinary simplicity, the brutality of the beating: two boys holding me up against the wall, and him, head down, pummelling away at my stomach. Not once but three times. Then the gig. The *aforethought*. 'Mum, don't throw any old fruit or vegetables away. I need them for something.' A bucket filled with apples, potatoes, tomatoes. But I watch him walk back down the shop, a long alley with stacks of amps on both sides, stopping halfway down to look at all the guitars hung on the walls. For an instant he seems wowed by the beauty and glamour of the electric guitar, its otherness to him. The bell rings as he leaves.

Later I realise he tracked me down in a town twenty miles away from where he lived, found the shop, walked in and apologised – a thing he'd decided to do, planned and executed. I cannot help but believe he overcame strong antecedent causal conditions to do this.

My father held decades-old grudges unto death, including against me. I have never held a grudge. Where would I hold it? I am, however, a bridge-burner. My funeral will be an intimate affair.

What I now know is that days after my mother finds out about the affair with Anne, my father says he will end it, that he doesn't want to break up his family. I am not sure how long this lasted, but he is back with Anne soon enough. Of course he is. He's unhappy with pretty much everything, but especially me. And he also senses my mother's allegiance shifting. She needs someone to believe in, someone who will reflect specialness onto her if he doesn't. At one point he blames her for siding with me, for ruining me. I hear this through the bedroom wall, sentences starting with 'That boy …'

One afternoon when I should be at school, I am home in the lounge listening to a record on my father's stereo. I've been dancing, miming guitar-playing, singing along. A slow song starts and I slump into my father's chair. Down the side, between arm and seat cushion, I find his diary. It is a long, slim rectangle, black covers, a week to a page. He mostly uses it for cricket matches (home/away), people coming around to buy ducks, social occasions, the odd police do. In the back there are phone numbers, a few addresses. I flick through. There is a lot of white space. I don't know why I stop where

I do. Perhaps my eye catches a different kind of entry. In the middle of a Tuesday he's written *I hate my son.* I close the diary and slip it back between the arm and cushion of the chair. It's not a shock, but I am numbed by it. The record ends without me noticing, and I sit in silence.

Over the years I have been asked why I think he wrote this. I think I've always known, but have found it hard to pin down. Erik Erikson said that it's much easier to disappoint our parents in *everything* than succeed in the *one thing* they care about. Which in my case was to be loveable. But that was impossible. So I offered up another way of having strong feelings towards me; that was my contribution. There was also his personality. He was sentimental, and this was a way of feeling sorry for himself. He wrote it in the same way a teenager might write something about their misery, the act of writing adding to the indulgence of feeling. Did he genuinely hate me? I don't think so. Was he prepared to find a way to love me, to be the parent, the grown-up in the room? No. I don't think so. Which is perhaps worse.

Influence

Over the next two years, I decide I must become an artist of some sort. This is based on encounters with certain artworks that I believe are speaking directly to me, as though I am their specifically intended audience. I have surges of unnameable feelings. I am a little manic when I try to explain how I feel. I believe my subjective experience must be the objective truth. I still have problems with this today.

Writing about responses to art, Christopher Bollas defines the 'aesthetic moment' as 'a caesura in time when the subject feels held in symmetry and solitude by the spirit of the object'. He then goes on to describe the nature of the relationship between mother and child as such an 'aesthetic moment'. It's as if he takes the adult experience of an intense aesthetic encounter and retrofits it to describe the quality of feeling of the primary encounter between mother and baby. Or, from the other direction (which of course is his objective), to claim that the *feeling of meaning* of an aesthetic encounter is derived from this primary relationship. What is interesting is the sophistication of the thought being used as a description for such a formative time. But what particularly interests me is whether in my case the drive to make art rather than just experience it comes from something lacking in the *feeling of meaning* from the primary relationship. After all, to produce something out of nothing doesn't point to a lack. But maybe emptiness is generative. Work made from it can feel full to others; for the artist it sits outside, and it can't do anything about the abyss.

I never saw either of my parents read a book. During the day they worked; in the evening they watched television; in bed they listened to the radio. When I was an infant my mother read to me from a single book of children's stories, under the title of each story a single black-and-white illustration, a woodcut. I never received books as presents. I didn't read as a child, ever. The only book I read as a younger teenager was a history of rock music told over a calendar year. I knew that off by heart.

The first novel I read is *Jane Eyre*; the copy I am given is a dull red hardback, its cover dusty as if it has been stored away since its original publication. We have a new English teacher, Miss Aspri. She is in her early twenties, dark, slender, pretty; I notice there is something sore about the skin on her face. It makes me feel strangely tender towards her. I read the novel to please her, to impress her; I want her attention.

At the same time we read *The Merchant of Venice* together in class, the whole play over a term, in thirty-five different, variously committed voices. We study passages in detail, index finger placed under each word, moving along the line as if we're learning to read again. Miss Aspri wants us to think about what is being said, expressed; she wants us to think about *meaning*. This is new to me. Most of the time I don't even follow what's going on. Others seem to find it easy, as though Shakespeare is written in modern English. But after a time, with Miss Aspri's patient guidance, meaning begins to unfold on the page, and a passage that starts like a piece of tightly folded origami reveals something else written on the inside. By the end of the term there aren't just words on the page but shape and sound, meaning and seeming, double meanings, ambiguity, even deliberate nonsense. It is a shock when you learn how indeterminate and flexible language is; I am surprised we are not struck dumb for a period.

By the end of his life Lacan was close to believing that the 'unconscious *is* language'. And at some point Heidegger moved from 'Language being the house of Being' to 'Language is an abyss'. I'm not saying I intuited this problem at fourteen, but I think Miss Aspri gave me a sense of both what language reveals and the bottomlessness of meaning.

After *Jane Eyre*, Miss Aspri hands round copies of *Sons and Lovers*. The covers are green; the pages are dry and browning around the edges. She tells us that when Lawrence wrote *Sons and Lovers* he wanted it to stand, among other things, as a testament to his mother, her sacrifice and aspiration for him, but also as a criticism of his father, in his view an ignorant and narrow man. Reading it later in life, Lawrence realised how manipulative and overbearing his mother had been, and that the novel was in fact a testament to the hard graft and gentleness of his father, a decent and good man.

I'm sitting under a low footbridge on the outskirts of Bromley at 2 a.m. It's rainy, damp and cold. I am with Roger, who is almost sixteen. He is large and round-shouldered, with big teeth and a loose, mobile mouth. When he speaks he uses unusual emphasis. Roger is popular, his company sought, his friendship the favour of a king. I have been chosen because I am the wayward son of the local police officer. He calls me Vic because being the son of a police officer is like being the son of a vicar. We are drunk on vodka and lime; I am so drunk I think I might vomit. Roger is telling me about this poet he pronounces *Yeetz*, who prophesied the end of the world when he stole a boat and sailed out onto a lake and feared that the mountain that reared into view would tumble down over him. *Yeetz* is a pantheist, he says. Roger declares himself a punk pantheist. Punk is a few years old now.

At school the following week I declare myself a punk pantheist to my form teacher, Mr Stewart. He asks me to explain. I mention *Yeetz* and the boat and the mountain and the end of the world. A day or so later, he squats down by my desk with two books and shows me how Roger has mixed up two poems and two poets. One poem is by Yeats ('Like Tom Yates'), the other is by Wordsworth. I pretend I know this, but I tighten up with embarrassment. He asks if I want to borrow the books. I don't. He closes each of them with a soft, dull clap.

Mr Stewart is in his mid-to-late twenties, a little squat, bearded, folky. He drives a green 2CV. He's been my form teacher for two years, but I haven't paid him much attention. Today, coming in from lunch, I see that he's sitting at his desk reading a book. I ask him what it is. He turns the book over to study the cover, as if he needs reminding. The cover has a photograph of a US American soldier's helmet with HELL SUCKS written on it. It's called *Dispatches*. It's about the Vietnam War, he says, by a journalist who was there.

I can't remember how, but I get a copy. I read it distractedly. It's not what I expect, whatever that is. Sometime later Mr Stewart gives me a copy of *Crime and Punishment*, a black Penguin Classics edition, a stencil image on the front of an actor playing Raskolnikov. I don't know why he gives me this book. I don't know why I start to read, but I do, sitting in a big ivy-green vinyl swivel armchair I found dumped on the side of the road. From that instant I want to be Raskolnikov. Who wouldn't? He's charismatic, brilliant, tortured. But it's not only Raskolnikov. I want to be Dostoyevsky. When I say his name I make the sound last as long as possible, stretching it almost to breaking point, *Dos-toy-eeee-ev-skiii*, like my mother does with the names of Italian actresses.

The next book Mr Stewart gives me is *Catch-22*. There is a moment when Yossarian, the main character, and another character, Clevinger, are arguing and Clevinger says, *You're no better than Raskolnikov.*

Who? Yossarian asks.

My hand goes up. *I know, I know – ask me!*

It doesn't matter whether Yossarian knows or not, and I realise now that he probably does, but in that moment he doesn't and I do, because last week I read *Crime and Punishment*!

What happened in those few seconds matters for the rest of my life. Somehow – and I think I only realise this now – it was about whether the self I had been constructing actually fitted me, whether I might give myself permission to become it, whether I could get away with it.

It's crazy, no? That in being able to answer that question I find proof that I am, must be, who I am pretending to be. But it isn't just that one question. Somehow there is something about the characters in the novels I read that year that set up orientation points to which I attach myself, and this allows me to create the shape I want to be. In short, I no longer have the desperate feeling of going about the world full of empty noise but am now a mixture of Paul Morel, Mr Rochester, Raskolnikov and Yossarian. A worrying quartet at the best of times.

Then one day Miss Aspri says, 'Today's homework is to write a poem about an animal.'

I can't remember the last time I did homework. But for some reason I do this, hastily, sitting in the corner of the sports field with my girlfriend T, using her back to lean on. It's about a parrot and it's in rhyming couplets. I read it out as I write. T laughs. I keep going. A day or so later I place the torn pages, folded and a bit scrunched-up, on Miss Aspri's desk and think nothing more of it. The following week she returns our poems. A lot of spelling is corrected, but at the bottom she has written, *You have a gift for poetry*.

First, I can state without equivocation that she is wrong: I have no gift for poetry. But she isn't *completely* wrong; I can write a bit. And this is the problem. If I've started to identify with characters in novels, I can now identify with the writers of those novels. Overnight, I decide I am a poet.

These days I wonder what would have happened had I not been able to write, had there been no correspondence between the noise I made and a way to shape it. Would the constructed selfhood sooner or later have collapsed like a dead star? Or, to use a less grandiose simile, return to its shapeless substance, like unset jelly emptied from a jelly mould?

But it seemed that I could keep up the pretence, the shape. It was a case of survival. I was a teenager living in a house of silence where only one person counted, and I needed to define myself in contradistinction to that person. And so, without resorting to a life of crime, what is more different from a policeman than a poet?

L.

I lose my virginity in a caravan in the middle of a wood. There are others present, sleeping behind a curtain that divides the bedroom from the rest of the interior. At some point there are screams from that section, followed by my girlfriend's face looking up in horror. We scramble into our clothes. It seems that a ghost has passed through the caravan, the torso and head of a man with a long beard.

We stand outside the caravan recounting what we saw, finding increasing agreement, a broadly similar image. I didn't see the ghost; I was looking the other way, down at my girlfriend. But I say I did. I saw Louise's face looking up over my shoulder, the change in her expression, then I turned around just in time. It doesn't matter whether this is true: I've lived with ghosts all my life, and I don't need proof.

Minutes later, we learn that a year or so ago the ashes of James's father were spread in this wood. He had a long beard. The ghost becomes him.

Some of us go back into the caravan to sleep. Others say 'no way' and trudge into the woods in search of the road and a long walk home.

My girlfriend and I split up a week later because I have been indiscreet; the story of the ghost is not the most interesting to a school year of fourteen- to fifteen-year-olds. A week or so later there is a pregnancy scare. I am not sure it's possible; because of the ghost we were interrupted and didn't continue. I try to explain this to people. It sounds stupid, even to the people who were there.

This first experience of heartbreak is telling. I will feel the same way a number of times in my life. The world becomes a vague, dreamlike place and I become weightless and drift, as if I've received a heavy blow to the head and can't shake off the effects. It's like falling in love, except the rejection feels absolute, a proof of something I already know, so I slowly disappear to myself, as if I only exist when constituted by another's focus on me. At this point I really am another.

There is a fancy dress party of some kind. My new girlfriend stands before me and with a delicate index finger pulls down my lower eyelid and applies black eyeliner. I am not sure who I am supposed to be – some kind of androgynous vamp? I am not displeased with the look. The next day I ask her to show me how to apply the eyeliner so I might do it myself. On Monday morning I am the first boy at school to wear make-up. It's 1980. I am sent home. I persist with the make-up and being sent home; I intercept letters to my parents.

What follows is a year of almost relentless bullying from the sons of local farmers. They don't like it that there is a boy in the year below who wears make-up and seems to have girlfriends from their own year. They punch me on the arm when I walk past them, knee me in the thigh at every opportunity. I don't care. It feels like proof of something: I stand out, I am noticed. I exist.

Then one evening, at dusk, I am grabbed and shoved into the boot of an American car and driven around for an hour. My back is imprinted with the tools I'm lying on. I can hear laughing. At one point someone shouts that they have a shotgun and that when they stop they are going to open the boot and shoot me. Instead, they pummel me, pull me out and throw me over a wall into a graveyard. It's dusk. I wait until dark and walk home.

I have a job washing dishes in the local pub on Friday, Saturday, Sunday nights. The local cricket team go there after home matches and my father is friendly with the owner. It is an early version of a gastropub. There is no dishwashing machine. In the kitchen, the plates, piled high, never seem to go down. The water is scalding. The steam heats up my face; sweat drips from my nose. I drink pints of orange juice and lemonade to cool down. As with most things, I learn slowly and then become proficient, after which I have ideas to relate that will improve the way I do my job. The kitchen staff find my presumption amusing.

One Sunday evening, the dishwasher before me hasn't finished his work and I am behind before I start. The dining room has been particularly busy and the evening sitting is going to be no different. I have an exam the next day; I cannot pretend to have revised, but an exam is an exam. I work hard all evening, but at midnight there are still dirty plates everywhere, including all the roasting pans. I explain, apologise and leave.

The following evening my father returns home in a fury. 'What have you got to say for yourself?' he says.

I can't think what he's referring to. I am scared and look at my mother who says, 'What's the matter, Mike? What's happened?'

He says, 'Be quiet, you.' She might as well not exist from that moment. He repeats: 'What have you got to say for yourself?'

I have no idea. I remember stuttering, 'I don't know what you mean … what …?'

He orders me over. Asks the same question once more.

I may be fifteen, but I am still a boy compared to this tall, broad man of forty-six. His size scares me. 'I don't know what you mean,' I repeat, but for some reason I add, 'sir.' He thinks this is cheek and slaps me hard across the side of the head. The impact is heavy and I fall to the ground. This isn't like last time, three years ago, after parents' evening. This time he hauls me back up, and with one hand holding me away from his body he hits me again, the same heavy, hard slap across the side of my head. Each time he lets me fall to the ground before hauling me back up, holding me there, slapping me hard. There isn't much I can do, so I let it happen. I am informed that he has good reason to do what he's doing. He has heard from the landlord that I left work early, which is to say I left work *unfinished*. I am being hit for two reasons. But the main one is my father's embarrassment. I try to explain: 'The other dishwasher … I had an exam …' He doesn't want excuses. This time he doesn't haul me back up but lets me stay on the floor and starts to kick me. This is too much for my mother, and she tries to intervene. He pushes her away and manoeuvres me out of the kitchen, into the next room, and closes the door, where he continues to kick me, really getting into it, low back lift, real power. I curl up, legs bent, arms around my head. My mother is now in the room, pulling him off. His exertions have left him out of breath. He tells me never ever to embarrass him again.

Later, my mother says to me, 'You bring these things on yourself.'

My father and I live in the same house for another year. We see each other. Not regularly, perhaps once or twice a week, in passing. We almost never speak.

I now realise my father was unhappy, confused, angry at the time. He hated his job, loved Anne, but felt a duty to his family. He was also used to the world bending to his will, and when it wasn't doing so, he looked around for someone to blame and saw me – the wrong son. But not only the wrong son. Someone who was so different from him, and therefore a kind of provocation. And this added to his sense of the world collapsing around him. In short, he was suffering his own existential panic.

Things Fall Apart

My sister is largely absent from this book. She was born fifteen months after me. We shared a bed until about the age of eight or nine. Not because we were short of rooms, but because I wanted to. I liked the warmth, the comfort of another's presence. Then one evening she slept in the other room, and that was it. I cannot remember playing together or having any shared interests. Two school years apart is a generation to a child.

Around the age of fourteen I started to hit her, always and only at the dinner table, and always only a sharp punch on the upper arm. I scared her into stillness and silence. I don't know how long this lasted. Too long. My mother always threatened to tell my father, but I knew she never would: she would never disturb his peace, nor did she want to be blamed for anything. My father was away most nights now, and there was no structure to the family. What was left was a total collapse of order, a kind of psychic free-for-all, as if none of us had any emotional constraints. There were other scuffles: me and my mother; my sister and my mother; the three of us. At one point, my mother was on the floor, screaming, and I realised she'd wet herself. My sister and I just looked on, turned away and went to our bedrooms. Once I tried to strangle my sister and my mother just looked on. No one knew what to do; what the rules were. Sometimes living in fear of something is itself an affordance, protects us from greater dangers. You can't remove it and expect life to be one big party: it's more likely to become mayhem.

Late summer, and a letter arrives. I open it walking from my house to my girlfriend T's, where I live most of the time now. I have taken a few O levels and a bunch of CSEs – I pass none. I scrunch up the letter and chuck it over a hedge. Am I surprised? I didn't revise at all, so no, not really. I think this outcome is worth scrutinising, though. I was reading a lot, writing a fair bit, not short of ideas about stuff. So why the total failure? I think it's because I didn't know what it meant to succeed at school. While I understood that higher marks were better than lower marks, why that mattered was a mystery to me. No one had explained that good marks were a means to an end. I think this is an example of the impact of class. If I hadn't been from a working-class background, my behavioural problems and academic failure would have been part of a conversation about *not getting into university*. It would have been explained that I was going to be denied this important event in life, and I would have understood that, even if I had chosen to ignore it. But I had no conception that there was an academic life beyond the fifth year at school. I don't think I even knew what a university was; I certainly didn't know what a degree was. I do remember a local girl disappearing to Scotland in the autumn and returning at Christmas, declaring herself to be a postmodernist, and I knew this was the result of more than simply going to Scotland. However, no one explained to me that this whole other world existed. That can't be the only reason I failed, though. It might have been that only one in seven eighteen-year-olds went to university at this point, but children from book-free working-class homes had been making that step for decades. And I can't deny that a couple of teachers were invested in me. Yet I walked out of the school gates at fifteen years old; I had no more thought of continuing school with a view to university than of becoming a soldier. And when I opened my exam letter, the information had no more meaning to me than if it had said I'd failed to become a soldier. 'We just expected to walk out of the school gates and onto the tour bus,' an old friend recently said to me. I suppose that's it, more or less; I expected that what I wanted to happen – to become famous – would one day happen. It didn't matter that I wasn't doing anything that would lead to that outcome. It is one of the terrible ironies of a constructed self that one has to believe in destiny, that the world will one day see you for who you are; after all, a constructed self is a kind of artefact in itself. While I am embarrassed to admit it now, I am sure that had someone asked me at the time, outside the school gates, why I should be famous, I would have looked down at myself and gestured: the answer was self-evident. It seems funny now, but I know that it was the beginning of something more problematic. Because a constructed self isn't real, it doesn't have the ego boundaries of a healthy false self, which means it doesn't know where the self ends and the world starts.

Around this time, my mother meets Toni, the daughter she left behind fifteen years ago. The reunion takes place at her mother's. I am there. I cannot remember much about it. I vaguely remember Toni coming in and my mother crying. Maybe my grandmother is standing there. I know that my grandfather, dying of lung cancer, was sitting in his chair struggling to breathe. The event didn't make much of an impression on me.

The Fall

I am coming home on the train from London, from a visit to the guitar shops on Denmark Street. It is an early autumn evening and is dark outside. The train is full. It comes to a stop at what should, according to my watch, be my station. The doors can only be opened by pulling the window down and using the handle on the outside. I do this and step out, but we're not at my station, we're not at any station. I step into sudden emptiness and fall. I seem to fall forever, as if there is no solid world. I might as well be hurtling off a cliff's edge at night, the rocks and raging sea invisible below. Then I hit a steep embankment, crumple up and roll down, bounce off trees, am jarred by roots, rocks, the contours of the sloping ground. I come to a stop in a muddy gutter between the slope and the broken tarmac edge of the road, at this time of the evening busy with traffic. I am winded and there is a sharp, hard spike of pain in my side. My clothes are covered in mud and emblazoned with autumn leaves; there are twigs in my hair; my palms are patterned where grit has imprinted itself and then fallen away. They are red and sore; I am sore. My body is thrumming with the initial impact, reverberating on the inside, as if my organs are somehow processing the shock. I cannot stand up. Car headlights sweep over me, revealing the treetops, then swoop away like searchlights.

I lift myself onto my hands and knees, then onto my

feet. I don't recognise where I am. There is nothing to do but walk in one direction and hope I am close to home. A mile down the road, I find myself at the small railway station before mine. There is a telephone box. I call T. She and her dad come to pick me up. How we laugh when I tell them what has happened. It doesn't matter how muddy my clothes, my stupidity: all we do is imagine the faces of the commuters as I stand up, pull down the window, open the door and step out. When we arrive home, T's mum runs me a hot bath. There is some supper if I want it, she says. She will heat it through while I get myself cleaned up. My girlfriend sits next to me on a painted chair, pulling the twigs out of my hair with one hand, collecting them together in the other. She washes my hair for me. Downstairs, I eat the warmed-up dinner. We then spend a couple of hours in T's bedroom listening to the first Psychedelic Furs album. I go to bed in the spare room. There are moments in my life of kindness, of bliss, of love.

Part Four

16–19 Years Old

Isobel

My first job after leaving school is working in a hairdresser's. It is noticed that I spend a lot of time looking at myself in all the mirrors, that I find a point on the shop floor where I can see myself in the round, as it were. It's not vanity or narcissism. One some level I'm always surprised to find myself there, so it's more like reassurance. It's why I need all the reflected angles – three dimensions are harder to dismiss.

The oscillations between waiting for fame and needing to remind myself every day that I exist seem to create a kind of surplus of energy in me, and it is pointed out that I shake. I am asked to stand still, to *try* and stand completely still. I can't. The shaking is most noticeable with a cigarette between my fingers or a drink in my hand. I am gently laughed at, gently teased. It makes me feel exposed, as if it reveals something about me that I can't hide, can't keep under control.

It's around this time I start to make grand claims about myself. I overhear myself saying, 'Sooner or later I will create a masterpiece.' I feel the energy causing me to shake, as if possessing its own power, telling me that *it* will produce something. That's the reason I can make the claim: I am not talking about myself – I am the energy's host.

In a street parallel to the hairdresser's, there is a second-hand record shop. I snatch glances at her: the back of her head, her hand taking a record out of the racks, a quarter-profile as she turns to look at the LP's cover. She is olive-skinned with dyed black hair backcombed a little, her fringe in her eyes. A few days later, I see her through the window, on the opposite side of the street. I watch her walk to the end and turn the corner. A week later she is across the road outside another record shop with a friend of a friend, and this is when I learn her name and where she lives. She wants to be an actor, I am told.

Over the next few weeks she is all I talk about. Before we properly meet she knows there is this boy who doesn't stop talking about her. 'He's obsessed with you!' everyone tells her.

When we finally meet, it is outside a third record shop; I am passing, and she is coming out. It's awkward. I know she knows; she knows I know she knows. Neither of us has much to say in the first few minutes, but neither do we make any effort to leave. After a while we find a mutual interest: our creative ambition. She is auditioning for drama school; I am writing a novel. Her mother is a writer, she says. She isn't particularly warm and makes it clear she doesn't want a boyfriend, but we become friends. Within weeks we are inseparable.

I describe what I feel for Isobel as *love*. 'Love at first sight,' I say, because it all happened in that first record shop – there, then, like that. But really I am beside myself with an all-encompassing lust: my body wants her body, and I believe that if my body has her body, something transformative will take place. It's as though she has a surplus of physical presence and that if she chooses to give herself to me, I will find my myself embodied in a way that has evaded me for so long. I basically think that Isobel, naked in my hands, will change everything. I even have told her that once. Her response was to desexualise the situation by saying, 'But if you think about it, aren't we just two blobs?' I think it can be safely said that our perceptions of what we wanted from each other were misaligned.

I do wonder whether we denigrate lust as an animating force, privileging the more mysterious and decorous 'love'. But isn't 'lust' speaking more honestly? After all, isn't it simply the unignorable, embodied expression of our attraction to someone? I mean, that's how it feels to me, and if I am to describe it this way, no one's going to say 'you just *think* you're in lust', as they did about my claims of love. As if lust is taken to be a confession of the truth behind the lie of love. Lacan is useful here. He takes what feels physiological and psychologises it as 'desire'. Although in this sense desire lies to us because it promises fulfilment if one gets what one wants, what it actually does is move on to the next object, because desire ceases to be desire if/once it is satisfied. In this way it is not dissimilar to the abyss.

Winnicott writes about the 'ruthlessness of the primal love impulse' in babies. I am certainly unrelenting in my pursuit of Isobel, and I cannot imagine a world where she doesn't finally give in. But I am not ruthless; I am kindly, nervily, charmingly attritional, looking to tire her out, wear her down. Maybe that's like a baby crying for its mother. Winnicott's mentor, Melanie Klein, might say that my infant fantasy of the 'good breast' was thwarted or unfulfilled and that for some reason this is the moment I've chosen to put that right. She might have a point. My desire for Isobel is voracious, as if I want to consume her, have her inside me. There is an obvious joke to be made here, but at the time it is no laughing matter.

Am I Mad?

My parents split up. It seems to happen in an instant. Without discussion or notice, as if we've all tacitly accepted that everyone will be happier.

My mother, sister and I move into a small end-of-terrace three-bedroom house. We aren't getting much of the family furniture, so a van is hired and we all pitch in, including my father. The last thing he says, after the final box is carried into the living room, is that if I ever need any advice I know where to go, and names Mr Stewart, T's father. The speech seems to have been rehearsed. He fluffs his lines because he really wants the scorn and resentment to land and puts too much into it. He needn't have worried: what else was I going to take from such parting words? At the door, he has one more thing to say. He can't resist. He tells me that I am to blame. 'This,' he says, looking around, 'is your fault.'

My father moves to a small house with four acres, about fifteen miles away. I see my father a couple of months after the separation. He tells me Anne will be moving in with him. Anne's love for my father is so deep it makes a mockery of my mother's devotion. It has religious zeal, the devotion of a disciple. It is ironic then that she is required to choose between my father and the Church. The Church agrees to annul her first marriage, but it will not countenance her marrying a divorced man. She is excommunicated. Only now do I appreciate what kind of sacrifice this was.

When Anne moves in, she brings her daughter with her. At eighteen months old, Clare is exactly the same age Toni was when my father refused my mother's request eighteen years ago. They are a happy family most of the time for the next thirty years.

My mother is just forty when they separate. She goes to singles' nights in local pubs and clubs and quickly learns who else goes to singles' nights: married men, gay men, and men whose wives won't do what they want in bed.

When the divorce comes through, she goes for a walk, sits on a park bench and cries. She tells me this and then starts cooking the dinner. I don't remember feeling anything.

For the next couple of years my mother is more friend than mother, our house more like a shared house than a family home. The front door is never locked and my friends come in and out; they become my mother's friends, and there is always someone sleeping on the sofa.

A shift happens during this time. My mother's devotion changes direction and my father's specialness is transferred to me. I become the target of her mythologising. My interest in books, music, art makes me different from other sons in the same way my father was different from other fathers. Her specialness now resides in a new kind of glamour, a kind of second-hand bohemianism I took from the Yateses a few years ago. She can finally be Maggie. Yet her devotion is not pure: it has another target beyond me, as it did when I was born. Except now I'm being used against my father, to prove him wrong. She can't live with the idea that he has both left her and might have been right about me, because that would make her a double failure – wife and mother – and this would mean she made the wrong decision in the beginning, including leaving Toni. And if this first decision was wrong, she would be a triple failure: wife, mother, mother. Fundamentally, nothing has changed: I remain secondary.

There are arguments with my father, in person, on the phone, when my mother says how I'll prove him wrong, that he'll regret not seeing what the rest of the world sees. There is an argument on the street that ends with my father driving off and my mother running after the car, banging its roof, screaming, 'He's a genius. He'll show you. You'll see.' The whole road hears it.

It seems that I no longer have to be perfect but a genius. It would be foolish to say that at least this time I have some control over the matter. Deciding to be a genius oneself is no more possible than being made perfect by another. But I do have some experience in pretence, of colluding with my mother to be something for my father. And my mother doesn't pick this story out of nowhere. I am happy to be called a genius.

There are times when I feel out of control. Like a child finding itself drunk. Moments when I want to bash my head against the wall and let out whatever's in there. Friends find me both compelling and laughable. But I am listened to, indulged. I am shameless. Even when challenged, asked what 'genius' things I do, I have an answer: 'I am a free artist of the self.' On some deep level this is the truth, given the circumstances, even if on a superficial level it is preposterous.

For a couple of months I find myself obsessed with reading Proust, and being someone who has read Proust, and disappear into my bedroom for days, hardly sleeping or eating; I steal the final volume from a second-hand bookshop because I've run out of money. When I've finished it, I seem to be locked in my own world, or underwater, and I can't quite hear people when they talk to me. When I try to explain why Proust is a genius, people lean away from me. I fear that what is happening to me is a kind of madness and that I will be permanently cut off from the world. There are other strange behaviours: I change how I look as I am seeking to find myself. For weeks I wear only black clothes, sunglasses indoors, walk with an ebony cane. Then overnight I slough off this persona and spend days in jeans and a T-shirt, walking barefoot outside in all weathers. I do not feel the cold and I stop in pools of sunlight as if I can't move onwards, as if the light is a sign of something bestowed upon me. Do I have delusions of divinity? I don't not have them. This period lasts a few months, and then it's gone. But people have noticed and are wary of me now; I am different in a way they find less fun.

Halloween

There are seven of us: Rat, Terry, Alan and someone called Podge or Splodge. There is Andy and Mick. We go into the woods with mushrooms and acid, our faces painted by Rat. We are psychedelic demons. Andy and Terry bring acoustic guitars; someone has pan pipes. There is an ebony chillum with a white stone bowl that Rat wants to 'christen'. We have a couple of torches and a yellow tin street light that flashes red. The mushrooms have been picked from a field nearby, hundreds of them, and semi-dried and parcelled in twists of toilet roll. They are easier to 'drop' that way; it avoids the truly retch-inducing taste – especially if you wash them down with a glug of something. The acid tabs are cut in half to go around. Rat does this in the wood, on the back of the guitar, with a penknife, someone holding a torch over his head. A scar is left in the varnish of the guitar.

For half an hour nothing much happens. We try to make a clearing between some trees, pull logs into a circle, light a fire. The chillum is filled. The night is cold and wet. Cloud obscures the moon; it's very dark where there is no light.

Then Alan says he can see a figure in the trees. It's too early on to claim that he's tripping, so we decide to look around. When we return, I notice Mick is gone. He's been taken, Rat says matter-of-factly. It happens, he says; Mick is now in a different realm, and it's his choice whether or not to return. When I look at Rat his eyes seem huge, his teeth bright, his tongue forked like a snake's – the drugs are kicking in. The torch beams move in slow motion and long twisting residues of orange light hang in the air. Snow has covered the ground and glisters in the moonlight. But there is no moon, just treetop darkness. Splodge or Podge suggests leaving before others are taken or decide for themselves to depart for the other realm; I agree. It begins to rain. Terry, the only one of us who is drug-free, says we're experiencing a collective bad trip and have to wait it out. But there is rising panic – Mick has been taken, Alan can still see a figure in the trees, and Andy is sitting cross-legged on a small island in a large pond playing the pan pipes. Where has the pond come from? How did Andy get over to the island? Someone claims that the chillum is still burning. It's a sign, Rat says. I want to go home. One by one the torches go out and the only light we have is from the flashing street lamp. No, not the only light: we are tripping and there are flashing lights everywhere: the air is full of floating glow-worms. Even the random notes from Andy's stupid pan pipes flash in the air.

I still can't believe Mick is not back. I tell myself he's gone somewhere to vomit up the mushrooms or fallen asleep. I insist that it's time to leave. Rat believes in the transcendent power of drugs, but also in their properties to reveal evil. He has questioned me: am I someone for whom evil is revealed by drugs? If this is the case for anyone among us, he says it will be me. This gives me status in his eyes, in everyone's eyes. When Rat decided we needed new names, *soul names*, I was offered Judas. After all, I was going to betray him one day. Making him Jesus, I guess.

It is raining hard now; thick drops bounce off the branches and land on our heads, running down our faces. It is very cold. Terry asks me if I want to jam. He's standing before me, holding out one of the guitars. He laughs; this is fun for him. We jam a lot, mostly extended improvisations around 'Hey Joe'; I hammer away at the chords while he plays the riff and solos. Next to us Podge or Splodge decides to strip off; it's the only way out. When I look back to Terry, he is gone, as if he too has been taken. It really is time to go.

I set off on my own but find Andy is with me. His face paint has mostly washed away and his skin seems beacon bright. He says he knows the way. Alan trails behind with Podge, who is naked, his clothes bundled in his arms. We meet Rat and Terry emerging from the woods. Rat is searching in his canvas satchel. 'What are you looking for?' I ask. 'More mushrooms,' he says. The ones he finds are sodden, and no one wants any.

We continue to follow Andy, and sooner or later we are on a road, under street lamps, the rain streaking down parked cars, glistening on the windows. I cannot believe it: we are back in the world. The real world exists, and we're in it.

It is only a short walk to Rat's. Our shoes are covered in mud, our clothes soaked through, our faces running with red and yellow paint. His father opens the door. He is a tall man; it is a big, smart house. We move past him, up the stairs and into Rat's room. Collecting up candles, Rat says we need to perform some ceremony for Mick. 'I'm heading home,' I say. Andy, who lives near me, elects to leave at the same time. Terry shakes his head. 'You go up together, you need to come down together.' I can still taste the original mushrooms in my mouth. Rat, going about his business, lights the candles and a few joss sticks while looking for his Tarot cards. If we stay, we might learn what happened to Mick, he says.

On our way home, Andy talks with great seriousness about what has just happened. The bad trip is a sign of some kind. In terms of loyalty, Andy is split between me and Rat. He's known Rat longer; he likes me more. He says he will report back tomorrow. When I arrive home, I find Mick drinking tea with my mother.

A week later, Mick, Andy and I form a band. Andy plays the bass, Mick is on keyboards. For the first few rehearsals I play the guitar and sing. We are then joined by two others, John on guitar and Martin on drums. We decide to be totally improvisational. I am no more tuneful than I was four years ago, but I am willing, and I seem to be able to summon up halfway comprehensible lyrics as I go along.

We rehearse in Andy's basement on Sunday mornings: two hours of non-stop improvised noise. We call ourselves Pure Absolute Noise, or PAN. Sometimes we're quite musical in a jazz-rock kind of way; other times we're like The Jesus and Mary Chain but without structure or form. When we really get going we produce an impenetrable wall of noise.

At one point, after rewiring his monophonic keyboard and linking it to a line of distortion pedals, Mick extracts sound I've never heard since, foghorn-like notes so deep they are a last warning: beware all, only suffering lies this way. The others try to compete; strings snap, drum skins split. I chant something or other, make noises, but in the end Mick takes it to a place where music ends, and I have to shut up.

We make tapes and send them off to record companies in London. One is returned with a personal message. There's no sugar-coating. *The worst one yet.*

There are times when I visit my father in his new house. I am picked up from the station, stay a few hours and then am dropped back and usually handed some money. I talk a lot when I'm there. I am full of myself still, the worst kind of person in his eyes, and yet I cannot resist. Sometimes I play him a recording of our rehearsal, both sides of a ninety-minute cassette. He listens. Given what I now realise we must have sounded like, this might be regarded as a kind of punishment. And in fairness he takes it.

The band play gigs locally and in London. We can be terrible: light, inconsequential anaemic noodling, as if we can't play at all. At other times the audience is left shaken.

A year in, there is a band meeting and I am kicked out. Not because I can't sing or because people are throwing vegetables at me, but because of my anger, which I take out on Mick, shouting at him during rehearsals, belittling him, bullying him. I don't recognise this. Andy tries to explain: 'You make everything about *you*.' And then just before he punches me in the face, Martin reminds me of what I said the day before when Mick talked over me. Apparently I stood there shouting, 'Don't you know who I am?! Don't you know who I am?!'

At the end of the meeting Mick says the equivalent of *Either he goes or I go.* They choose him. I am surprised, but I don't care.

It has taken until now, almost forty years later, to understand how my behaviour must have seemed to everyone around me during that time. I had no boundaries. It often felt that there was no world beyond me, the world *was* me – I felt limitless. I never stopped to think about anything I said or did; I expected everyone to take it and come back for more. Except you cannot be as difficult as I was without sufficient talent and get away with it. Yet I often did get away with it, so it was not an easy lesson to learn. 'If you can't fight, wear a big hat,' my father used to say. I was always in a fight; my personality was my big hat. Martin didn't need a big hat: he broke my nose instead.

Isobel II

Two years after I first saw her in the second-hand record shop, Isobel and I go out for the evening, and she comes home with me. We stay up most of the night talking, and at five in the morning she accepts my invitation to get into bed, at least for a little warmth and comfort. She stays the next night, and the next. For a couple of weeks, we exist only at night. We leave the bedroom at dusk to forage in my mother's kitchen. We eat foodstuffs raw and cold from the fridge, drink straight from bottles and cartons. At dawn we are exhausted and fall asleep in what seems like the boundless room of my single bed.

We move to London. Her father, a journalist, has a run-down one-bedroom flat in Gloucester Road, when Gloucester Road was itself a bit run-down. It is large and light, with a small rooftop terrace visible through the bathroom window. It is summer in the city. I don't remember a rainy or overcast day. Isobel works as a hairdresser's model during the day and takes acting lessons in the evening. There is an old manual typewriter in the flat, and I start another novel.

I am not wrong about my lust for Isobel. In bed, especially in the afternoon light, what is empty in me *feels* full. More than that, I overflow – a physical sensation from deep in the gut. I understand the inclination to give the experience a more metaphysical cast: as the gut rises in its fullness, it is taken up by the mind and there seems to be the creation of something numinous, as if love is being made and must spill out. It doesn't matter that Isobel doesn't love me (she doesn't); her body is what I want. And in the moment it is given to me, I feel rid of the deprivations.

There is a small bookshop on Gloucester Road. I browse often, seldom buy. There is a small book, discounted. *Existentialism and Humanism* by Jean-Paul Sartre.

> *What is meant here by saying that existence precedes essence? It means that, first of all, man exists, turns up, appears on the scene, and, only afterwards, defines himself. If man, as the existentialist conceives him, is indefinable, it is because at first he is not something. Only afterward will he be something, and he himself will have made what he will be.*

On reading this I should have been able to breathe more deeply. It was after all a vindication of everything I thought about myself, my role in my own making. But this wasn't the case; for the next few years I was breathless, desperate for everyone to recognise that this act of self-creation was a fundamental truth about me. It also means that I doubled down on my right to be myself. If that's possible.

After six months of living together, my desire for Isobel ends. It falls off a cliff. One moment I constantly want to devour her, and then … nothing. Lacan has much to say about this. Firstly, desire is the desire for nothing nameable, so it was never about Isobel or even her body. Most tellingly, though, Lacan says that what is desired can never be found because the object of desire isn't actually an object but a space around which we move in a state of desiring, with the sense of satisfaction like a mirage that we only learn doesn't exist when we arrive close to it. And there I was, certain possession of Isobel would create deep bodily satisfaction, that she possessed a plenitude of pleasure that would keep me full forever. Whereas instead I was left with a new sense of emptiness, of desire hollowed out.

But none of this means that I am not devastated when Isobel leaves me. I go home to be looked after by my mother. I can't leave my bed. I am an invalid, a neurasthenic. I want to be placed in a turn-of-the-century sanatorium, wrapped up in expensive blankets, fed clear soup in the thin air. When I stand I am dizzy. I seem to have no centre – stomach, gut, groin have gone – and I fear my bottom half will collapse to the floor and my torso float away.

I return to Proust, the great psychologist of obsession. I have this mad notion that if I can master the long sentences myself and write of Isobel as he writes of Odette, Gilberte, Albertine, I will have gained something from this, that I might win Isobel back. It is as if art possesses its own mysterious force of attraction, and if I send her what I write she will feel compelled to return. But Proust is easy to parody, and parody is an extra-special kind of insult to something one loves. All it creates is another kind of broken-heartedness.

Part Five

20–29 Years Old

Mirror Phase II

I drift for a few years. It doesn't feel like it; it feels joined up – teleological, with something transformational always on the verge of happening, to prove, I think, that the world is just. For two years I go back and forth to Paris, staying with a girlfriend in Belleville, and write a novel, visiting Proust's grave for inspiration. It doesn't help; the novel is terrible.

Back in London I am part of a band that has some success. We have residencies, fill mid-sized venues, record companies turn up to gigs. Most of the time I am the logistical engine behind the band's success, yet I fear being kicked out, as has happened twice before, and become easily angry, demanding, absolutist. When things don't go my way, there is a kind of brinkmanship involved. Do you dare ignore me? It is exhausting for everyone around me, and so by the time I'm twenty-five, when friends are getting married, starting second jobs, buying flats, I am unemployed and homeless. No one will employ me because I'm not qualified to do anything, and I'm not fit for labouring, although two weeks' roofing proves my lack of fitness for such work. There is night work at a plastics factory, where I am fired for being too slow. Then a burger bar, which lasts a little longer. Finding somewhere to sleep each night requires calling up people from phone boxes, hoping to catch them in, begging for favours, otherwise it is a night wandering the streets. It doesn't happen often, but there are some grim hours spent on benches in parks or stations trying to get comfortable and keep warm. I am chatted up by middle-aged men who offer me a place to stay. When I decline they walk off, but they often return to see if I've changed my mind, or just talk to me, interested as to why I am sitting on my own at this time of night. There is even one possible job offer, if I promise not to say anything about how we met, until it transpires that I'd need to learn to drive a coach. But inevitably someone else catches their eye and I am left to myself. I'm once joined by a girl and we take it in turns to rest our heads on each other's shoulder. She is nervy like me and chain-smokes roll-ups. She tells me about being pushed out of her family home in Wales by a stepfather. Her mother begged her to stay, but what was the point, she says – it was a shit place to live anyway. We fall asleep together. In the morning she is gone.

In a large, shared house, there is a big mirror in the bathroom that seems to have some strange power – when I look into it, I cannot avoid seeing something I'd rather not see. The image in the mirror seems clearer and more present than it ought to be, and this makes me, standing opposite the reflection, seem insubstantial. With my hands on the sides of the sink, I lean in, look right into my face. The image is not unfamiliar: a man in his mid-twenties, longish dark hair, blue-grey eyes, a thin, sharp, pale, unshaven face. But there is also another image there, more strangely familiar: of a small boy, round-faced, freckled, fringed with black hair. The little boy's presence is making something known to me: you are not what you think you are, who others think you are, and because of this you are scarcely anything at all – this is the cold hard truth.

It is so disturbing I want to collapse onto the floor and be found there by the next person who needs the bathroom. And not to be found as the twenty-five-year-old simulacrum of the grown me but as the small boy in the mirror, and to be taken to a place of safety. There is no one to find me, though, and there is nowhere to be taken.

I return to the sitting room, to watching TV or listening to music, to cans of lager, cheap wine, roll-ups and spliffs. I sit there until the last person goes to bed, usually past 2 a.m., when I make up a bed on the sofa only to be woken around 7.30 by the first person who gets up for work. If someone stays at home for the day I can hang around, otherwise I need to find somewhere else to go.

I secure a year's flat-sitting gig in Battersea, high up in a tower block, on a large estate. I spend weeks alone. The only people I speak to are the cashiers in the local shop. I sleep for long stretches, but it isn't restful. Every two weeks, Tom comes round, bringing beer. Once a month, Curtis visits and we go to Brick Lane for curry. In between, I read and write. For long stretches of time I feel suicidal. Curtis insists I see my GP, and I am referred for a psychiatric assessment at Springfield Hospital. The psychiatrist, who doesn't seem much older than me, asks me whether I might be bipolar. He genuinely seems to be asking me what I think. I don't know what this is, so I say I don't know; I don't think so. He prescribes me old-school-style antidepressants. Then, as I'm about to leave, he asks whether I want to voluntarily commit myself for further observation. I decline.

The antidepressants make me lethargic and agoraphobic. A local mental health nurse visits with a leaflet of charitable psychotherapy institutions. The first clinic with an available appointment is in West London. I am so broke I have to walk there – over an hour and a half. At the end of the session, I'm asked to make a donation. I break down and weep. The therapist gets up, leaves, and I am left to cry myself out. A month later, I am offered ten sessions of psychotherapy at six on a Wednesday evening in a small room at the back of Chelsea Old Town Hall. I'm required to pay £1 per session. The quickest route from the estate to King's Road is to cross Battersea Park diagonally. It is autumn and the park is locked at sunset. I find a tree I can climb that allows me to drop down the other side of the railings. At the Albert Bridge end of the park, I need to climb out beyond some wrought-iron spikes embedded in a pillar and swing around onto the road. When it's high tide, the Thames isn't far below, a green-grey churn, but it has a sense of substance, as if it would suck you down.

The therapist I've been allocated is in his mid-thirties, tall, with dark hair and a short beard. He has an accent I can't place. I spend the first session talking about my father. At the end he says: 'This has nothing to do with your father, it is all about your mother.'

I lose confidence in therapy for decades.

A friend comes round and sees the state I am in and arranges for me to stay with his parents in Wales for a few weeks. They own an independent bookshop and I work there in the mornings. In a back room, there is a piano. When there is no one in the shop, which is often, I sit at the piano and bash at the keys as loudly as I can, indiscriminately, randomly, but with as much rhythmical propulsion I can muster. I feel a strange euphoria, as if the noise is connecting me to something alive in me. With the sustain pedal down, the noise fills the shop and becomes a kind of self-generating harmonic cloud, and with it my body disperses into a million pieces and forms into waves of overlapping sound. At one point I am tapped on the shoulder and a middle-aged man asks me casually, as if I'd been sitting at the front desk, 'Do you have any James Bond?' I shake myself free of the music. 'Unfortunately not,' I say. 'The owners are Marxists.'

I go back to London.

The same friend introduces me to Francesca. We like each other and go to art galleries, sometimes the theatre, or just for a walk. She is at law school during the day; in the evening she works in a bar in Notting Hill. When I meet her we share a bottle of wine, our elbows on the table, and smoke. She likes me, she says, but she is in love with someone else, a married man; if it wasn't for him she would be with me. A few weeks before Christmas we kiss on the top of a double-decker bus, then she has to leave for her shift at the bar. She has green eyes and I send her a poem by Baudelaire. On the phone she tells me it is better in French.

The week before Christmas she and her flatmates have a party. Halfway through I learn she has a new boyfriend, someone from law school. It seems that everyone knows. I leave and start to walk home. I feel as if there is a crack somewhere deep within me and that any knock from inside or out will cause me to shatter. The cold winter air feels equally fragile, like the thinnest glass, and if I gave it the gentlest knock the world would also shatter and fall at my feet and there would be nothing.

What does it mean to feel that the world is just a picture, to walk into what you perceive as a two-dimensional representation, and for it to remain so, despite the three-dimensional activity of walking *into it*? I now know that this is called dissociation. But if you believe that knocking the air in front of you means the world will shatter and fall into the abyss – that might be diagnosed as psychotic. But what if there is a fundamental truth to all this? Maybe the world shatters before us more often than we like to believe, and it's simply that the pieces are big enough to be put back together quickly, without us really noticing.

I stay in the flat over Christmas. I forget to eat. My depression deepens. I curl up in bed, knees up, arms around my head, gripping it, pulling it tight in. The dose of antidepressants is increased. All that happens is I feel increased levels of anguish, as if the depression was protecting me from the real pain. At one point the pain feels unbearable, which is to say, I can imagine it as life-ending. A notch more and there will only be one way forward.

Escape

After months of not seeing my father, we are sitting around the dinner table eating a takeaway curry. Conversation is polite. Anne is a little nervous, hovering, asking every few minutes 'Is everything all right, Mike?' to which he replies in a jokey, slightly irritated voice, 'All right, my love' – a catchphrase from a 1970s comedian. Anne's daughter Clare is about eleven.

We are in the middle of eating when I say it. I don't know why I say it. There is no plan to do so – it just comes out. I hear it as if spoken by someone else, a version of me sitting in the next chair.

What I say is this: 'My therapist said that the reason I talk too much is because you didn't talk to me as a child.' I say it conversationally, like I might have asked if he'd seen a particular comedy I knew he liked. As if it is something that might be discussed over the chicken tikka and lamb madras.

Anne places her hand on my father's thigh. Clare continues to eat. My father brushes Anne away, stands and says, 'I'm too old for this,' and leaves the table. Anne goes after him, through the hallway and into the lounge. I follow her. He is sitting in his chair, large hands on the arms, big bald head looking straight ahead. I have met this version of him before.

She kneels beside him, hands clasped over one of his knees, looking up. She is asking if he is all right. He refuses to speak, just looks straight ahead. I am now in the middle of the room, using the heel of my hand to wipe away tears. I am not quite crying: tears are flooding my eyes but somehow not falling. I can't see my father because of this flooding. I am aware of my reflection in the dark windows.

Anne looks around and glares at me. *Why did you have to say that?* I recognise this expression from years ago, when my mother and father arrived back from that parents' evening, except this time Anne is on my father's side in a way that makes my mother's devotion to him seem partial in comparison. But then I am not her son.

My father then speaks. 'How much?' he says. It's not obvious what his question is referring to.

Anne says, 'What, Mike?'

He won't repeat himself.

'To go to America,' a little voice says.

I look around. Clare is standing in the doorway. Of course. America. While Anne was setting out the food, I'd said a friend wanted to go to New York to work for the summer and I thought I might go with him, but before the conversation went any further, Anne was in the lounge door, on tiptoes in her ballet pumps. 'All ready, everyone. Everything's ready. Come through.'

So I name an amount and Anne fetches a chequebook. My father then drives me back to the station. When we are parked at the station entrance, I try to lean over, as I always do, to kiss him. He remains upright in his seat, no give in his body, no pretence at love. He wants rid of me.

To New York

We arrive in New York on 3 July 1992 and stay in Alphabet City, at that time a neighbourhood of crack dens. 'Don't go out after dark,' the woman in the ground floor apartment warns us. All night, fireworks are rolled under cars and alarms set off. There is gunfire and police sirens. The next day I walk to Greenwich Village, Washington Square Park, up Fifth Avenue. The weather is hot, humid, overcast, rainy. I don't get what's so special about this city.

I find a job and a month-long holiday let just north-east of Chinatown, the top floor of a five-storey walk-up. My job is to watch New York area TV news and summarise coverage of the 1992 presidential election. I am working illegally. My shift starts at 4 p.m. and finishes at midnight, during which time I watch six hours of news, madly typing what is being said about the election, which is everything, all the time. After work I get the subway to TriBeCa, in those days a desolate part of the city, and meet my boss at the North River, a huge and mostly empty bar. The bar staff are old guys who've quit high-paying jobs so they don't have to pay their ex-wives alimony. Twice a year they and some of the regulars go to the Dominican Republic and sleep with sex workers for a week. It's an unprepossessing place, but somehow this is where I find myself. Among this crowd no one cares who I am, what I think, and no one is at all interested in my genius. It feels like a doctor has recommended two years in New York instead of bed rest.

In Chinatown, I sit on the fire escape drinking grape juice. I watch a gunfight: three men moving between parked cars and shooting at each other. I know I am supposed to go inside to avoid a bullet ricochet, but instead I crane my body over the ironwork to see more clearly.

One night during my first winter I am mistakenly arrested for holding up a bodega. I am walking along the street, vaguely aware of some shouting, when I am I pushed into the fruit racks outside a grocery store, told to put my hands behind my head and a gun is pressed between my shoulder blades. Another night at the North River, a police officer draws his handgun on me; he thinks I've been hitting on his girlfriend. Apparently she pointed in my direction when he asked her where she'd been. A month later I am in a car crash at 3 a.m. on an off-ramp from Manhattan into the South Bronx. My boss is driving, stupendously drunk. For some reason we're heading to his mother's apartment. A taxi pulls up and the driver orders us to get in. He looks at us with fury: a few more minutes and you'd all be dead, he says. We drive blocks and blocks under an overpass. A whole desperate world is living there: the taxi is pelted with rocks, there are gunshots.

One midwinter evening I almost kill someone myself. I am cycling down Amsterdam Avenue, all the lights are in my favour, and I am picking up speed. I have cycled down here every day for a year; I know how fast it is possible to go before the first red light needs to be anticipated. But then out between two parked cars steps Philip Glass. He looks at me. In the microsecond before I hit him I see on his face a realisation and acceptance of what is about to happen. No panic. Just a taking in and processing of this catastrophic moment. I am doing the same. This is where it ends. But I manage to swerve. Given the speed I am travelling at, and the distance between us, it shouldn't have been possible to both miss him and keep the bike upright; at best I should have caught him in the ribs with my handlebars, taking the bike out from under myself, my body surfing down the road. But I both miss him and stay upright, and Philip Glass lives to continue his trilogy of operas based on the work of Jean Cocteau.

A year into my stay, I am sitting at the breakfast bar in the apartment. While I can't see the front door of the apartment from where I am, I find I am picturing it in my mind's eye, and beyond it, the short hallway to the elevator. It's in this instant I realise something. No one's going to leave the elevator, walk down the short hallway, knock on the door, and because of my innate talent made known to them via the cosmos, commission me to write a novel, a novel of genius, that will then be published to great acclaim.

I should perhaps state this again: it is only now, aged twenty-seven, that I realise that this is *not going to happen*, which means, logically, that some part of me thought it might *really happen*. It's not that I believed that I didn't need to produce stuff along the way, that I required being discovered first, like a young person picked off the street to be a model. But I did believe that something of genius from me was inevitable, and if it wasn't forthcoming, the world would come looking. Sometimes the floridity associated with psychosis is only an inward experience.

At work I recount my revelation to my colleagues Kevin, Melissa and Mason. They agree it is indeed unlikely that anyone is going to turn up on that particular errand, given that no New York publisher knows who I am or where I live. They don't seem to question my claim of genius, but neither do they confirm it. They are in two minds. Melissa, who is ambivalent about me, says I *seem* like someone who might be a genius. She then ignores me for the rest of the week.

I buy the first ever Apple laptop. From mid-morning to mid-afternoon I sit at the breakfast bar and try to write. Or I sit in Central Park, Bryant Park, Battery Park and try to write. Or I sit in diners uptown, midtown, downtown drinking coffee, trying to write. But I write nothing I can bear to read back. I delete everything. I watch the grey cursor working its way backwards, eating up every word.

Kevin, originally in New York to study painting, decides *he* wants to be a writer, and brings work in progress to the office and reads it to us. It's an impressive rip-off of early Cormac McCarthy – emotionless descriptions of men going only by their surnames, wandering deserted places. I go back to imitating Proust. I seem to be able to write about anything in the style of Proust. It's extraordinary how much time one can waste writing endless sentences that amount to nothing. What becomes plain is that I have no story to tell.

I have a go at writing poetry. It confirms what I've always known: there isn't a word of poetry in me, despite Miss Aspri's claim.

Kevin writes poems and reads them to us. They are work-overs of Beat tropes, New York dives, bums, ferocious women screaming in the streets. I worry that Melissa thinks he's more talented than me. I worry that he's more talented than me. Mason even says it straight out; of course he does.

Kevin is fired. It's partly my fault. The boss asked about his work habits and I told the truth: he was always late, didn't finish his work, and often left early. And I am glad he's going; I know that Valarie, another colleague, is likely to be given his shift, and when I work with her and Mason at the weekends we never stop laughing – we are like a little family, and when we're together I am happier than I've ever been before or since.

It's time, though, to leave New York. My boss has a drinking problem and is running up bar tabs all over town. My flatmate is getting married and needs me out of the apartment. I make a half-hearted attempt to rent a room but I cannot afford anywhere safe. When I see a room in the low 100s in the Upper West Side, I am told not to go out after dark if I take it. It's just like my first night in the city.

I fly home in early 1994.

I was happy in New York, at times joyously so. I was comfortable not being from a place. I liked having to explain myself, even if the story was that I needed to find somewhere I felt at home and that I'd discovered being elsewhere was the key. I called my parents twice in the two years. I hardly ever thought of them, as if the distance between us made a difference, their existence thinning out over the Atlantic Ocean, fading to nothing miles before I reached Long Island. I felt parentless in the same way I felt without a meaningful history, and so it was possible to leave things behind and start anew. And New York is endlessly distracting: there is no time to look inward, especially if whatever you might dwell on isn't driving you forward to the next distraction. New York won't let you settle, and in that sense I felt an alignment with the city. If at times I felt a little weightless, more often than not I felt in wonderful, precarious balance and that anything might happen around the next corner. Who wouldn't want that? It was beautiful.

Hypochondria

I rent a one-bedroom flat in south-west London. The idea is to write something, anything, to have something concrete to send out into the world. It doesn't matter what happens next. If nothing: write something else; send that out. But before long I become unwell again. It's not depression this time but a kind of highly focused, compressed mania. I am convinced I am dying, that I have an organic condition that will kill me soon, if not in days, then months. I visit Tooting Library's medical section every day and spend hours sitting on the floor surrounded by medical dictionaries, looking up the symptoms of cancers with a prognosis of high mortality for a man of my age. For a time I settle on pancreatic cancer, but soon my focus shifts to HIV/AIDS. It's easier to ruminate on why I might be HIV-positive: a blood test in Senegal, unprotected sex in New York, a date with a woman who confessed to recreational heroin.

In his paper 'Fear of Breakdown', Winnicott writes: 'When a fear of death is a significant symptom [...] the patient has a compulsion to look for death. Again, it is the death that happened but was not experienced that is sought'. He later suggests that fear of death is the fear of the psychic death of the infant, something which has already happened and which he calls the 'primitive agony'. It might also be the case that a fear of death is also the truth of not having felt fully alive, and I am looking for my death to make sense of this: death is coming to claim what is already the case. Freud believed that the final objective of the death drive is to return us to the nothingness from which we emerged, that as an organism we possess a trace memory of non-existence, and that the death drive wants to take us back to that state. Along with many others, I don't think this is right. Sometimes I feel that I am teetering on the edge of an abyss and know that the tiniest miscalculation will tip me over and I will plummet down. It's not the death drive that will make this happen; it's an insufficient hold on life.

Should I die at twenty-nine, as I am convinced I will, I will have amounted to nothing and proved my father right. I find this so traumatising that I cannot eat. I weigh less than nine stone.

It is my first Christmas back. It is expected that I go 'home'. I will spend Christmas Eve with my mother, Christmas Day at my father's with my sister, her husband and their two small children, and then return to my mother's.

I am low when I arrive at my mother's house and go straight to bed. The next morning I give my mother her present. As usual she finds it difficult to show any pleasure and examines it as if she can't understand what went into the decision to buy it for her. As if she believes it was chosen too quickly, that I should have put more thought into it. What she says is that she doesn't deserve such a nice present and sets it aside.

At my father's I try my best to be engaged, but it's a strain and so I follow instructions, go through the motions. The present-giving is all about the children, two and four years old. I have bought them what I was told to buy; in the same way, I receive CDs and books I asked for, and an envelope of money. I say thank you, but a grandchild runs up to my father to show him something and my words are missed.

Shortly before lunch, a friend of my father's comes up the drive, a famous actor who is around my age. My father leaps up, calls out to him, thrilled. They hug in the doorway. The actor stays for twenty minutes. He is warm, kind, charming. We hear a lot about his current work, a new TV show, a feature film.

I do my best to be jovial at lunch, pull a cracker, read out the joke, wear the paper hat, but I struggle to say the right things and the table often stops and looks at me. During the afternoon, I read while others play games. It is mid-evening when we leave. I sit in the back of my sister's car, jammed between two sleeping children.

A week later my father calls me. He never calls me; he believes it is the duty of children to call their parents. For a second I wonder what's wrong. His voice is cold and deliberate, rehearsed: 'I just wanted to say that you ruined Christmas with your moping. You ruined it for the children, for Anne. Did you bother to think about all the hard work she put in to make it a special day for the children? How dare you. Who do you think you are?'

I hang up. We don't speak for two years. But his voice is in my head once again.

I hear from my sister that my father and Anne are going to Goa, a place they will now visit every year, until he dies. This doesn't make sense to me; I've never known him leave the UK. Soon they are going twice a year. Over time my father becomes like a benevolent emperor visiting a distant colony. In comparison to him the Goans are small, so even grown-ups seem to flock around him like children. Everyone knows him; everyone feels known by him. Years later, Anne will tell me that when he arrived at the airport he made sure he said hello to all the taxi drivers. At the hotel, before he went to his room, he visited the waiters and kitchen staff, shaking hands, joking around. Then on to the beach to see the vendors. No one was missed out. He and Anne brought gifts from the UK, but his largesse was his presence, the attention he bestowed. There are lots of photographs of him from Goa, drinking, dancing, relaxed and happy among locals and other tourists. I do not recognise this man, but I suppose I envy him.

For months I suffer from a kind of inertia. I don't need impending death now; I am dead inside, and that'll do. If I am not sleeping I am watching TV in a stupor. I have no energy to read, seldom go out, don't answer the phone. I know this can't go on, and so one evening I drag myself to A & E. Part of me wants to be put into some kind of indefinite coma;

at least I'll be medically supervised rather than waste away alone. And who knows, when I emerge I might feel better, reborn or something. This is the dream as I wait. This is what I'll say if they ask me how I can help.

A junior doctor tells me to see my GP. I don't have one, I say; it's why am here. I'm given a leaflet and told not to come back unless I've had an accident or it's a medical emergency. The following morning I walk to the nearest surgery and sign myself on as a patient. I say I can't go home; I'll wait for whoever becomes free. There is no pushback; the receptionist makes me a cup of tea. At one point she sits next to me and tells me about the village she's from in Ireland; she is going back there soon and invites me to visit her.

The GP is tall and handsome, sixtyish, with a neatly trimmed beard. He has the bearing of my father but with a different kind of sternness, as if he could also be kindly when it mattered, serious but approachable. There is a collection box for a local mosque on his desk. I tell him how I am feeling. He listens carefully, then takes out a large book from a glass bookcase. It is like an ancient book of spells. For a second I think it's the Koran. He lays it on his desk and opens it. I am asked a set of questions, and at each answer he turns a page. He doesn't look at me.

Half an hour passes. The receptionist comes in and asks if everything is fine. The doctor raises a polite hand and asks me more questions. His finger moves down the page. One more question and he stops.

He writes a prescription. I am told to return in six weeks.

At the chemist's I learn I have been prescribed a homeopathic remedy, a small white pill, containing the essence of phosphorus, to be taken once a day. On day five my mood lifts, my mind becomes clear, hours pass without a thought of symptoms. Maybe it is magic. Real magic.

On day six all my fears return. I keep taking the pills.

Six weeks later, I go back. The doctor is dead. The nurse tells me he had cancer; his decline was quick. Did he prescribe himself homeopathy for his cancer, I wonder.

The new doctor asks me whether I've heard of Prozac.

'In a couple of weeks you'll feel completely different. Better than ever. Just you wait.'

Writing

I move to a friend's empty loft in Hoxton, pre-hipster days, and start a novel. It's the first thing I've written that seems to have a sense of itself – or at least no sense that all I have read my entire life is Proust. I work hard, seldom go out, my mood is good.

Then one day I meet an old friend on the street who invites me to party the following Saturday. I only decide to go at the last minute. When I arrive, the first thing my friend does is introduce me to a woman, Bridget.

There are times when God or the gods, or fate, fortune, destiny, or even the determinist principle of cause and effect (i.e. it was meant to be) bring into your life the person that becomes your life. This is Bridget in that moment. Do I recognise it as such a gift? Yes and no. Certainly by the end of the evening, after a party in a warehouse, walking back to my loft at dawn, I am convinced of something. It must be similar for her, because we spend what feels like all day every day, every evening and every night together for the next three months. I love her masses of blonde curly hair spread across my pillow, her willingness to listen to me talk but endlessly interrupt, the way she wants to hold me in order to fall asleep. There is one morning when she wakes up and, naked, shuts the full-length windows, and for a second she is a silhouette against the dawn light, long legs, high bottom, slim hips, slender shoulders. 'Wow,' I say, and she laughs. We laugh a lot. It seems that finally I can make someone happy who also makes me happy.

At which point she returns to her ex-boyfriend.

I start seeing Joanna. We are a little combative, but she is a person of seriousness, of intellectual and creative integrity. She believes in me. For a year I am split between Joanna and Bridget. Bridget comes around often; we have a lot of fun, which is not to be underestimated, but she is still with her boyfriend. The relationship with Joanna feels more like a creative project.

I feel blessed, greedy; I want them both. Meanwhile I keep working on my novel, finally landing an agent with Joanna's help, at which point we split up.

There is something about having an agent that feels like I'm in the world for the first time. There is someone working on my behalf when I'm in not in the room. It's not just me and the work; it's me, the work, and another in the world.

The novel is sent out and an editor at Little, Brown wants to commission it. My agent says they are discussing an advance of £10–15,000 but that I'm not to spend the money yet; there is the formality of the weekly editorial meeting.

There are only a few times in my life when I feel on the brink of transformation – transfigured, even – like a god radiating light in a William Blake illustration. Each of these moments, and I can count them on one hand, comes with a phone call from a woman about my writing. I feel that I learn something about myself: I'm not wholly mad thinking I can write; it's not a symptom of my ongoing madness in search of a true self; I haven't misconstrued the evidence to fit the story. And so at these points I don't need to be a genius, only someone who's written something another person wants to publish.

A few days later, my agent calls. She can't understand what has happened; it's never happened before; she's never heard of it happening before: 'Marketing said they "don't know how to position it". Whatever that means. But they've passed on it.' No other publisher shows any interest. I am desolate for a few minutes, angry for hours, then I fall into a deep sleep lasting two days. When I wake it's like it never happened. What I think is: *Fine. I'll write another book.* And so I do in a concentrated frenzy. It is finished in a month. My agent hates it. I am thirty years old.

Part Six

30–51 Years Old

Settling Down

After a dinner party for her thirtieth birthday, Bridget stays over and never leaves. Within months we talk about having children. Bridget is dispositionally happy, a sunny person. If Schopenhauer is right and we seek partners to correct or balance our attributes, will this, I wonder, make our children more emotionally stable than me? I think I say this to her.

Bridget meets my father on his sixty-fifth birthday. He takes to her. Despite the stories she has heard from me, she confesses that she takes to him. He is handsome and good company, she says; it cannot be denied.

A number of people suggest that there has been a change in me. Bridget has changed me. There is even reference to an 'old me' and a 'new me'. I am calmer than I have been most of my life, and it's true that the love I feel for her isn't desperate in ways it has felt before, and the fun we have, how we talk all day every day about books, philosophy, TV, becomes part of my love for, and helps me trust her, and start to believe in, if not directly feel, her love for me. So if at times I am unsure, even doubtful of her love, it is equally clear that what we have is special, a match that couldn't have been found with anyone else, and that feels like a gift of the gods.

But I am not fundamentally changed. My need to be the centre of attention still often means I don't care what I say to people, who I make uncomfortable, who I hurt. Bridget says: 'It's like you turn into another person - you don't even look like you.' Within a year we lead separate social lives. At times I wonder why she doesn't leave, as if our connection is as unstable, fragile as the world often feels to me. I tell myself that maybe what makes me who I am at my worst has its attractions when I am at my best. And maybe there is a little more balance these days. What I don't get and never really do is that she is committed to me, partly because my behaviour has always been a good excuse to kick me out of the band.

It is the hottest summer on record and the hospital has no air conditioning. Bridget is having another scan; they are weekly at this point, as one of the babies is not growing as fast as the other. We are taken to see a consultant. He starts by telling us how special our babies are. Bridget disagrees; they are no more special than other babies, but the difference is that they are ours. He wants us to come in tomorrow so Bridget can be induced.

The following day we are driven to the hospital with a friend and shown to a very hot room. We are told nothing will happen immediately and that we can go out for coffee. I call my father to give him an update. He is brusque. It seems I have done something wrong. I work it out: I haven't called him over the past few days. Given his heart attack a month ago, I should have called to check up on him. My inclination is to hang up, but I don't. I try to explain: it's been a difficult week, it's going to be a difficult few days, and then there will be two babies, and he has Anne, Clare, my sister looking after him. He doesn't say anything to this. I say I will let him know when the twins are born; it will be sometime soon, maybe even today. I then call Anne at her work, something I've never done before. She says, 'Don't worry. When I get home I'll give him hell.'

Everything that can be done to induce Bridget is done in that hospital without air conditioning. The outside temperature is in the high thirties and feels hotter inside. Over three days and nights we have six different midwives. Consultants enter the room with dash and discuss within earshot what they are planning next. They do not directly inform us of anything, but whatever is decided on there is no downward movement: the twins are not ready to make an appearance. Neither of us sleeps for thirty-six hours.

At five on a Monday morning one of the babies is showing signs of distress, and it is decided that Bridget will need an emergency Caesarean. We are taken down to the basement. The operating theatre has air conditioning; it's like walking out of North African heat and into a hotel room. Bridget is terrified and begs me to stay next to her and keep talking. She is so exhausted she is barely conscious; she says, 'I just want them out and to go to sleep.' The procedure takes place behind a curtain arranged over her belly. I stand by her head repeating, 'It'll be all right, it'll be all right.'

One baby is removed and handed over to a nurse. A few moments later, the second appears. Both babies are long and thin and dripping with pale blood; each cries within a few seconds. I am told Bridget has lost more blood than is usual and that a transfusion might be necessary. I go over and see the babies, swaddled in towels and wearing little knitted caps; their tiny faces are pale pink and I watch their fingers and toes curl and flex. I can't really *see* them. For a moment I think they are identical.

Something appears to be wrong. A small old woman, an orderly of some kind, is cross. She wants attention. There are whispers, more discussion. I ask what's wrong; I am clear-voiced and confident. It turns out that a swab is missing. Thirty were counted out at the beginning of the procedure, and there are now only twenty-nine – one must have been left inside Bridget. The consultants are only partway through sewing up the caesarean section; they seem at a loss as to what to do and want certainty from the orderly. Did she originally miscount? This is not a question she can reliably answer. I ask about options. Swabs have a metallic strip woven into them so they can be seen by an X-ray machine. Then X-ray her, I say. Bridget is too weak to be moved, though, and the only portable X-ray machine is in another building. The only other option is opening her up again, but she's already lost a lot of blood. The room is silent. How long will it take, I ask, to get the X-ray machine here? They are unsure. They huddle and discuss, still can't decide.

I'm beside myself with tiredness, worry, confusion, but I've also had enough. I move to the centre of the room and say, 'Listen!' Then: 'This is what we're going to do. You will order the X-ray machine now and sew her up while it arrives. You'll then X-ray her and decide what to do based on the results.' One consultant goes to a phone on the wall and the other works on Bridget. A nurse comes over and asks Bridget whether she wants to hold the babies. She shakes her head: she just wants to sleep. The nurse returns with both babies in her arms, leans down so Bridget can at least see their faces. She closes her eyes and turns away.

While we wait for the X-ray machine, I wander back and forth between Bridget and the babies. The babies are very funny-looking, I tell her, but she seems barely conscious. I stroke her forehead, her damp hairline. After twenty minutes or so, the double doors of the operating theatre open and the X-ray machine is wheeled in. It is the size of a small tank. The consultants position its long arm over Bridget's belly and adjust the camera node so it's flat against her skin. Non-essential people, including me, have to leave. It doesn't take long. A couple of minutes later the images arrive. No swab.

The first night after the babies are born, Bridget wakes at midnight. She gets out of bed and in a daze pulls the tubes from her arm. She doesn't notice blood gushing out and all over her gown; all she wants is to see her babies. She doesn't remember that they are in the basement, and she wanders the hospital looking for them. I have carried this image within me ever since. It breaks my heart.

Returning home the first night, I vomit and then cry. I cannot stop crying. There is no thought attached to it, just an outpouring. I don't for a second think what it means for me to be a father. That comes later, weeks later.

The following morning, I receive a letter from Anne. It is four sides of small blue notepaper. She pleads for me to apologise to my father. She must be going through a bad time to ask this of me. Of my father's feelings towards me, she writes: *There is a lot of love there.* I realise she can't bring herself to say *Your dad loves you very much* or even *Your dad loves you*. She has removed the subject and object from the sentence. It's rather neat. I admire her honesty.

Fatherhood

After a week in the special care baby unit we bring the twins home. It immediately feels as if we have two new flatmates; they already seem like people with characterful wills of their own. Winnicott was right: a baby is a person.

I take three months' paternity leave. During the day this mainly consists of Bridget and me walking for miles with the babies in slings. At night we lay awake, feeding them on demand, which feels like all night. Six months in we are so sleep-deprived that something needs to give. Midwives offer advice about what to do, mostly involving the babies crying for different durations. We try every version, even though we're looking for consistency. Some nights we leave the twins to cry themselves out and then get them up when we can no longer take it; other nights we get them up straight away, change our minds and put them back to bed, listen to them cry and then get them up again, achieving nothing. Having twins isn't double the work of a single baby; the work is squared. One baby is exhausting, while a second baby is exhausting when you're already exhausted.

Those times I am alone in the house, I don't have the energy to make it to anywhere soft and lie down on the first piece of empty floor. I am so tired I become irritable and angry, then ill. Once a week I sleep downstairs with earplugs in, but I still think I can hear the babies crying. I watch Bridget being an uncomplicated, loving mother, giving everything, delighting in everything – so much more than 'good enough'.

I take it for granted I will be an improvement as a father, but I also worry that my selfhood isn't robust enough to hold back the force of the antecedent causes that will inevitably darken everything, that if my mother and father brought their grief and guilt to their parenting, I will bring the damage that parenting caused, and on and on. What am I doing bringing more life into the world, I ask myself. *Why* do any of us do that? How dare we make more life and force others to live it! If asked I would insist that I love them both, but I don't feel completely connected; it's as if I meet them afresh each day and need to learn to love them each day, and sometimes I fail and they seem like strangers.

I go back to work. I fall asleep on the train in. I can't read, think, write. I drink coffee all day and feel discombobulated, irritable, overwhelmed.

Freud claims to have suffered from stomach cramps after visiting his father, and I experience something similar. The visits themselves are generally OK, but during the drive home, my gut spasms and I am in excruciating pain for most of the journey. I usually go straight to bed, even at four or five in the evening. One afternoon, the babies won't settle in the car, or when we get home, and I am exhausted and in pain. I feel resentful. Everyone else seems to take such simple pleasure in the babies. I feel deprived and at the same time emotionally besieged, as if I can sense everyone's need for me to be the father I know I can't be. I feel weak and pathetic. Sometimes I lose my temper. It's my way of coping: to wear a big hat. But that isn't an option with babies. They don't care how big your hat is.

It's a Sunday morning, the babies are a few months old, and we're all together in our bed. Wilder is fractious, her limbs flexing. The signals are clear: she wants to be picked up. Macleod is lying between us, quiet and dreamy. Bridget dandles Wilder: she is happy, her face is alive. Glancing from one baby to the other, I realise that Macleod is never going to demand attention in the same way, send the signals. But this doesn't mean he doesn't want attention. I decide it is up to me to make sure he receives it. I realise I have a role, a job to do, a duty. I reach over, lift him up, sit him on my lap, and I know in that moment that I have made a commitment to him: if it's not his way to show what he wants, he will not be left out. We will not treat his mysterious tranquillity as convenient in these early days of exhaustion.

Drugs

My first novel is published when the twins are three years old. 'Is it going to be one of those books everyone talks about?' my mother asks. When I go to my father's house I notice that the copy I sent him is on the bottom shelf of the bookcase behind the sofa. In setting the bar for success so high, my mother has increased the probability of failure; my father has hidden me away. It seems we cannot help being ourselves.

The novel is well reviewed. It makes it onto a few minor prize shortlists, wins a minor prize. Sales are low. I deliver my second novel. A year later it is published, to mixed reviews. Sales are non-existent. Then I receive a telephone call: the novel has been shortlisted for the Costa Novel of the Year. Is *this* the moment of transformation I've been waiting for all my life? I am exhilarated and decide that now is the time to write the long novel I've been thinking about for some years. It will be set in Argentina and deal with the fallout of the Dirty War, the Disappeared, tango, and *Tristan und Isolde*. I take the family to Buenos Aires for eight weeks. What I write over the next year is an unpublishable mess. I do not have the technique for such a sprawling narrative. I do not publish anything for another twelve years.

I have been off medication for eight years, and I start to withdraw into myself. There doesn't seem to be much of an outside world, just vague movement, muffled sounds. I feel as if my mind is being wrecked by an invisible storm, but my body behaves as if the ship is in becalmed waters. Exchanges with Bridget and the twins are automatic; I seem present, but I am pretending. I pretend I am working, but instead I spend all day, evening, the middle of the night, once again researching high-mortality cancers, only this time I have the internet to help me and have no need of a library. I begin to count down the days before I am given a terminal diagnosis. When I look at the twins I feel deep sadness; I truly believe they will be without a father in months.

I make three appointments over three days with three different doctors. At the third one I break down. He writes a prescription. 'These are good for ruminations,' he says. A week later I say to Bridget: 'I am never *ever* coming off these drugs.'

I become a firm believer in what I call my 'head meds'. This is partly because without them I don't connect my depression or hypochondria to anything in particular; when I am not taking anything, my narrative is all about dying, and when I take the meds, it feels like nothing is wrong. Also, I am very anti-therapy. It doesn't help that my only encounter twenty years ago was unsatisfactory, but it seems that most people I know who've been in therapy for years are unaltered. But there is another reason that I refuse to even entertain the idea of therapy: I don't believe there is a therapist alive I can't out-think. This is my MO, the proof of who I am – I can out-think anyone. Ironically, there is a kind of truth to this. Not that I can out-think every therapist, but that I'm so well defended I'm not sure even the most gifted therapist can make a dent in my defences. And if they do, I will quickly construct a narrative that means I can dispose of them. Maybe I have to believe in my head meds because they are my only option.

My stepsister, Clare, is getting married. My father becomes withdrawn. It seems Anne is spending a lot of time on the arrangements and he feels abandoned. He writes the only email I ever receive from him. Anne no longer loves him any more, he says; he tells me that she is going to leave him. The message is ridiculous and full of self-pity, but he has revealed something about himself for the first time. I reply and tell him not to worry, that I'm sure everything will be all right.

Anne takes my father to the doctor and he's prescribed antidepressants. It becomes one of the only things we ever have in common. He takes them for the rest of his life, and there is no doubt that over the next twenty years he's more content than at any time in his life – more patient, less irritable. Even over the last five years of his life, during three bouts of cancer, he is more good-natured in his exchanges. But he always makes sure I know what's what. 'Those children better make your life hell,' he laughs. His laugh is mirthless.

Diagnosis I

Only days after the twins start nursery, Bridget and I are taken aside.

'Macleod … seems very isolated. Have you ever thought he might be autistic?'

We are shocked by the baldness of the assertion. It's almost like gossip between parents. We ignore it. Yes, he does sometimes seem separate from others; he does possess a kind of mysteriousness. But he's a happy child, with no developmental or intellectual difficulties.

Within weeks of Macleod starting reception, this 'isolation' is mentioned again. There is a small garden next to his classroom and he likes to walk around and around it, talking to himself. He often leaves the classroom alone and is found there. We are told that he isn't making friends like the other children; he doesn't join in. 'But it's more than that,' they say. 'It's a sense that …' and then they stop.

In Year 3 he becomes very unhappy. It's the first time he's had an unsympathetic teacher: she wants order, compliance and attention, and he wants to be at home, head on the carpet, at the level of his Lego, looking at the action up close, dreaming of battles between intergalactic forces. The teacher tells him off; he sits under the table and refuses to come out. When we can get him to talk about school, he is certain and fixed about what he thinks is unfair. He sees the world as direct cause and effect, without context or other viewpoints. When we meet with his teacher, she is similar: she won't listen to explanations, and context is irrelevant. She wants him to behave, which means doing what he's told. A week later, he hits her.

The school advises us to have Macleod assessed. I don't want this. Like many parents, I don't want *difference* to be turned into a diagnosis; I don't want my son to be defined by a diagnosis – his behaviour will no longer be idiosyncratic but autistic. Bridget overrules me.

He is described as high-functioning, lively and bright. At one point he's asked to describe a colour and he says 'Grey-y white' and I hear the clinician say, 'I haven't heard that before.' He does everything they ask of him obediently and curiously. I have no idea what will happen. I don't want my aversion to labelling to disadvantage him in the near future with help and support at school, but I don't want a label to disadvantage him later in life, where it might preclude him from certain careers.

It takes only a couple of weeks before we receive the assessment. He is diagnosed with autistic spectrum disorder and given a full statement of special educational needs.

When I tell my father he says, 'It makes you love them more.' And when we next visit, Macleod is given extra attention – nothing compared to Thomas, my childhood friend, but it's noticeable. My father calls him Macca, which irritates me.

Wilder notices the extra attention her brother receives, the extra focus, the leniency, especially from me. Bridget insists that we can still be fair to them both, by which she means treat them equally. I don't think that possible. It's not a zero-sum game, but I accept that Wilder will still lose: there will be times of unfairness that she'll have to live with. That's what she gets out of this: a loss that isn't compensated for.

She watches me at dinner. 'Daddy always serves Cloudy first. Gives him more.' When she and I are talking and Macleod walks in, she notices that my attention switches. 'I haven't finished, Daddy,' she tells me. And when there are arguments between them, which there will be with seven-year-olds, she says, 'You always take his side, even when I'm right. It's not fair.'

Her solution is to test me, test her brother. She starts to goad him in front of me and watch me judge her for it, tell her off. She wants the evidence. And I provide it.

When we're alone Bridget says, 'She fears you love him more.'

I am categorical: 'I don't, I really don't.' But I know I am gentler, more caring with Macleod; I give in more quickly and find myself wanting to protect him. And if you take what this must look like and transpose that into the feelings I must have, Wilder can't help but think I'm being loving to him and tough on her. There is also something so grown-up about her expressions that I treat her as if she were an adult and her brother a child – an adult goading a child with additional needs. This makes everything worse; I am sharper, less sympathetic with her. Bridget and I argue fiercely. Wilder hears what is said and takes from this that there are sides: Macleod has Daddy; she has Mummy.

I know I am not getting it right, but it's not that I'm not trying. Yet in the middle of these bursts of anger both mother and daughter look at my face and see something *unloving*. To me it's only fleeting. Whatever my feelings in the moment, there will be a cascade of other emotions later on, which will include infinite love for, and wonder at, a little girl whose smile can transform my mood in a way nothing else ever has. But I don't realise that this isn't enough. It doesn't restore the balance, because my daughter doesn't see my inner world.

Diagnosis II

My father has been in the hospital for a week; the doctors aren't sure what's wrong with him. I visit him every other day. He rolls in and out of consciousness and complains that his head is hot. I sit next to him and use a small sponge to squeeze drops of cold water over his head. I hold his hand. I choose to; it's just lying there, and I grasp it. I don't feel anything apart from the size of his hands, which seem to come from a different kind of human: Ozymandias, Zeus.

The doctors say most of his discomfort is from dehydration, but he will only drink cold orange squash, and only from a glass. And not any glass. He requires it to be thin-rimmed, small and light in his hand, held between his giant fingers. I buy him liquorice because I know he likes it. On the drive home I fantasise about his death. I hope he will die soon. I want to be free of him. I tell people this, and also that when it happens I will feel nothing.

Eventually they open him up and he is diagnosed with lymphoma, a cancer easier to treat than some. He will likely respond to chemotherapy, they say, but the cancer is also likely to return. If he remains strong, treatment should work a second time, but not a third. No one says it, but it's a 'three strikes and you're out' situation.

For the next year, my father is too weak for visitors – the cancer, the chemotherapy, generally having to shift his bulk around in such a depleted state – and I don't see him much. Anne seems to have a surplus of strength: running her shop, looking after the ducks, attending to his needs. I am aware that he suffers terribly: bouts of vomiting, diarrhoea, falling over and not being able to get up, sometimes spending hours on the floor until Anne arrives home. There are times when I think he might die from the side effects of the treatments; I expect a phone call any day. When I hear Anne's voice I'm almost giddy with excitement. But it's just an update. The tone of her voice, always so full of love for him, suggests I must feel the same.

I am working on a new novel about a man not unlike myself, with a family not unlike mine, who fears an authentic encounter with God. I feel that I have a sense of how God's grace works. I see this as separate from a belief in God, which is not a question that interests me. We are at the height of New Atheism, and people around me seem to think I'm going through a conversion experience. It's binary: Dawkins or God. I say I'm not clubbable in that way. I don't regard this novel as in any way connected to my father or his death. It doesn't occur to me that what I am doing is preparing a replacement for him.

The rows with Wilder, with Bridget, with Bridget and Wilder, become worse. I am full of fury, resentment. I lose my temper in ways that frighten them. I slam doors, punch a wall, smash a rickety wooden chair on the floor. I want to be what I imagine they think I am: a monster. It's easier to disappoint than succeed, I reason, so why not become the worst version of myself, but this time as a parent to a child? I know I'm opening the door to Wilder feeling similarly towards me as I do to my father. Although this door is only open a crack, I'm not doing anything to close it. There is no wiggle room; I can't stop myself, it seems.

If I'm honest, I have another much more solipsistic concern. I will be fifty next year, and something doesn't make sense. It's not a question of sequence, as if fifty shouldn't come next, though I don't think fifty *should* come next. I now experience a different kind of anger. The trigger isn't out in the world – other people, obvious frustrations – but a boiling-over deep within me, as if the abyss has now become something volcanic. And once it wants to make itself known beyond me, it can't be resisted. I shout at colleagues, friends, even lose my patience with clients. I fear turning tables over in public and only just leave rooms in time. Something is horribly wrong. I ask myself whether it's really to do with my age or the fact that I have taken the wrong route to get here. This is what it feels like: as if at some point I took a wrong path. But surely that's the opposite of what happened. When I separated myself from my parents' world, I was striking out on my own path, the right path. Although it might not have taken me quite where I want to end up, or expected to end up, I made my own choices, and achieved a few things along the way. Yet right now my life feels like it's flattened out to a bone-dry desert where there is no feature on the horizon and to walk in any direction is to walk forever.

Fifty

When working from home, I wake up, see the children off to school, answer urgent emails, then am back in bed by 9.15, half-reading, half-dozing, half-dreaming. When I drift off fully I dream deeply, always finding myself in a warm, light-filled place of safety. If I wake, I pull the duvet over my head and return to my dreams. At midday I answer more emails, eat some toast and Marmite and walk the dog. By 2.30 I am in bed again, reading, drifting off, dreaming. The children come home from school and I go downstairs. Macleod walks around the kitchen table a few times, as if he has something he wants to say, then goes upstairs to play computer games. Wilder wants to talk about her day in detail. I can see that she resents me holding her off until her brother has gone, but we won't see him until dinner, whereas she and I will spend the entire time together. While I make dinner we discuss Shakespeare, films, music, the evils of social media, her friends, her teachers. I am often spellbound by her insights, her cultural sophistication compared to me at her age. Sometimes we even dance. There is no way this is a repetition of my relationship with my father. These late afternoons are my evidence – what I point to when my love for her is challenged. But it's not enough, I am told. She needs to *feel* I love her. I can't bear this. I feel hurt, resentful, cornered.

The problem is that I have no sense of what it feels like to live in a loving home, with loving parents. I can see that both children are comfortable being at home, in this home, even when I'm here. When they walk into a room I am in, nothing happens; they don't tense up, look for an excuse to leave, they say 'Hi, Dad' and go about their business in our house, *their home*. Not only did I never have this, I don't have it now; I tense up and want to make an excuse to leave the room. For me, having a child and parent at home together means there is something at stake. And I cannot learn anything from my children, cannot adjust myself because they feel a comfort I don't. This is a developmental problem from childhood, what Winnicott describes as learning how to be loved whatever the circumstances. It's why I can be irritable and impatient and they can still wander around the house at ease – they were loved more or less in the right way at the right times.

Three

My father has been in hospital for a few days; tests are being done. Anne calls. There has been an accident. He tried to get out of bed, felt dizzy, fell and hit his head. The doctors describe him as 'very poorly'; we should come to the hospital as soon as possible. When we get there, he's sitting up in bed and seems well. I think to myself: he will live forever.

A couple of days later, Bridget and I are by his bedside. He is chatty – he always likes to see Bridget. The consultant comes in; it's a second recurrence of the lymphoma, she says. 'What happens next?' my father asks. She explains that if he chooses treatment and it works, he might have three months. He immediately spots that this will include Christmas and seems pleased by this.

'And if the treatment doesn't work?' I ask.

The consultant's expression is caring, gentle, but resigned to the facts. 'Three weeks.'

'And without treatment?'

She turns to my father. 'The same,' she says, 'but you might be more comfortable.'

My father doesn't appear to be in shock. There's a strange matter-of-factness in his manner. When the consultant leaves he talks about making it to Christmas, as if that's all he's heard. You can't blame him. Three months is the classic cancer prognosis, but three weeks? It's all but here. Dostoyevsky was right: give a man a choice between death and spending eternity standing on a narrow ledge, and he'll choose the ledge every time. My father chooses treatment.

My father remains in hospital for a week. Anne stays with him every night, sleeps on a blow-up mattress next to him. She stays, the nurses tell me, the most nights of any relative ever.

The treatment doesn't work. A hospital bed is delivered to my father's home and placed in the lounge. A few hours later, he is brought home by ambulance and moved onto the bed. He can see the ducks through the large windows. Each day a hospice nurse visits to adjust his pain medication. Anne sees to all his other needs. If one were counting down, he has two weeks left.

I visit every couple of days; sit by the bed. He asks after the twins and Bridget. Everyone is fine, I say. I ask who's visited. He tells me.

He seems at peace. Anne will certainly have talked to him about entering heaven and being welcomed by God, and in the past he would have rolled his eyes at such talk, but I suspect he takes comfort from it now. I ask him if he's scared. 'It can't be too difficult if so many people have managed it,' he says. It's not a joke. He is reassuring himself that nothing is required; he's too weak now to want to produce effort of any kind.

There is one night that delirium and cramps from the morphine take over and Anne calls me to say the end might be soon. But the following day my father rouses himself a little and says he feels like a bottle of beer. Anne looks on the television for a cricket match being played somewhere in the world, and they sit together and drink a beer. It is only one day until the three weeks are up.

I continue to tell anyone who will listen that I will feel nothing when my father dies. I am sure of this because I feel nothing while watching him die. When my behaviour towards him these past weeks is pointed out, I explain that I am being dutiful, and being dutiful is not a feeling.

Two days later, around 4 p.m., Anne asks my father if he wants the TV on. *Pointless* is about to start, she says; he likes that. She stands facing the TV, the remote pointing at the screen. The opening music plays. She turns the volume down a little. Behind her she hears an intake of breath. Later she will say she somehow felt a stiffening of my father's body and knew there'd be no exhalation, as if he simply couldn't manage it one more time. He has lasted one day beyond the three weeks.

Part Seven

52–53 Years Old

Full/Empty

His head is slightly rocked back and to the side, his skin thick and sallow, mouth dropped open a little. He is the first dead person I have seen. I peer at his face and wonder whether what is absent might be visible somehow, as if something about the aspect of death in a face will tell me something about life. But it's only internal chatter. I don't really think anything. I take two photographs.

Anne and I sit in the small dining room and drink tea. I am sad for her. I can feel through her what it means that he is dead, this man she loved as deeply as I can imagine love being felt. I suppose I catch a glimpse of what it might be like to feel loss in such away. But there is no grief. Nothing comes in waves. I leave and drive home.

Freud is at his most illuminating on mourning when he says that 'no aspect of the loss is unconscious'. He goes on to describe a category difference in melancholia, where there is an 'unknown loss', adding that this leads to an 'extraordinary reduction in self-esteem, a great impoverishment of ego', and concludes that, 'in mourning, the world has become poor and empty, in melancholia it is the ego that has become so'. It is this latter state that we cannot defend ourselves against, because our selfhood is in peril from within. Sitting in the dining room with Anne, I don't imagine for a second that my father's death will have this effect.

Anne asks me to write and deliver the eulogy. I am the eldest child, a writer. I suppose these are good reasons; I can't think of any others. I've written many different things, but not a eulogy. For a while I am well and truly blocked. I need a structure of some sort, but what? I need, in old-fashioned storytelling terms, a character arc. In the end I tell Anne that the eulogy might contain a few critical references to his relationship with me, because I want to tell the story of how he grew into his role, that with Clare and his grandchildren he became wiser, more forgiving. 'Only good things!' she says. 'Only good things!' She is adamant. I push back a little, and she blames me for what went wrong between us, says that I'm going to make the eulogy about me, like I do with everything. It gets heated, acrimonious. I back down, but I will give Dorothy and Michael, my mother and sister their due – I am not hiding them away. With surprising good humour, Anne says that there are people in the village, including the priest, who she will need to inform in advance; they don't know anything about my father's past life. To them, she and Clare were his first and only family.

The church holds about three hundred people and is full. There is a breakout room with a video feed – also full. A livestream is available on the church's website for those in Goa and around the country unable to make it. I am aisle side in the second row. When called upon, I walk past the wicker coffin and up to the lectern. I begin.

'A year or so ago, my father said if he could have his time over he would have chosen a slightly different path, and with a wave to the window with one of his huge hands, he explained he'd like to have spent his whole working life running a smallholding like his home for the last thirty years.

'It is true he found certain aspects of his years in the police force distressing. But what a loss it would have been for others. He claimed it was all a big mistake: a day trip during National Service, and then somehow he found himself reporting for training at Hendon. I maintain that it was exactly the right career for him. My father was a public servant to his core. He was from a generation where duty was its own reward. But what he offered the public was more than doing his duty; for those who required it, he was generous with his time, a patient listener, thoughtful with his advice, and never quick to judge, especially with young people. While his moral compass was perhaps fixed from a generation ago, it didn't prevent him accepting that the world changes, and how we live changes with it, and he remained until the end a wise counsel for whoever wanted it.

'The one time my father's life intersected with world history, it had nothing to do with local policing or sage advice but a variety performance given by policemen and their wives to raise money for a police charity, given at the then New Theatre, Bromley. It was produced and directed by my father, with my mother Maggie as lead dancer. My father's big turn was a Shirley Bassey impression. How did this intersect with world history? Well, here.' [I hold up an edition of the *Daily Sketch*.] 'For those who can't see, on the front cover we have a picture of the first man on the moon and next to it my father directing several policemen in the "Dance of the Cygnets". It was an enormous success. Personally, I wished it had led to a life in the theatre, but it wasn't to be.

'The three constants in my father's life were children, waterfowl, and cricket.

'As a natural leader of men, he invariably became the captain of any cricket team he played for. His commitment to the game never wavered – he played into his sixties. His great love was for Kent and England. During the Seventies, when we attended games together, Kent was going through a purple patch; not so England. At home, we knew his mood was governed by England's performance.

'Ducks were his great passion. From a birdwatcher as a child, to a smallholder in his middle years, in later life he became the president of the British Waterfowl Association, a not untaxing position.

'And then there were children. He was born in Dover, the eldest of six, and as the story goes, when at eighteen, pushing a pram with his youngest sister Jackie inside, most people assumed he was her father. Then came his own children; in his twenties, Michael, who is no longer with us; in his thirties, me and my sister, Sarah; in his forties, Clare. His late fifties saw the arrival of grandchildren, Michael and Zoe first. My twins, Wilder and Macleod, arrived in his seventieth year, and then Clare went one better with three grandchildren, adding Polly, Freddie and Jessica.

'It says something about the love his daughters felt for their father that both named their boys after him – he was Michael Frederick.

'I'll now share memories passed onto me from Sarah and Clare. When my sister Sarah was nine, our dog Fred went missing one morning. It was a school day and our dad was in his uniform ready for work. Sarah was beside herself with worry. My dad told her to go to school; he was sure Fred would be at home when we got back. Just after the start of school, Sarah was called into the headmistress's office. She thought she'd done something wrong. Our dad was there to tell her that he'd found Fred – he'd been killed on the road. My dad understood it would have been worse for Sarah to spend the day at school worrying, only to find out when she got home that her dog had died. He didn't postpone the news for his own sake, as he so easily could have done. There are few harder things than telling your child their dog has died. And for a man who cared deeply about punctuality and his civic responsibility, he understood some things must be done, even if they make you late for work.

'On a lighter note, Clare remembers his reputation with boys at her school as a formidable obstacle to expressing their affections to her. Not only did a myth arise that he walked the perimeter of the grounds armed with a shotgun whenever a boyfriend was in the offing, but it seems he really did intercept all her phone calls, delighting in telling any boy who called that she was out with someone else. But then a daughter will always forgive a dad that bought her a horse for her thirteenth birthday!

'In many ways, Michael and Zoe got the best of him: content in retirement, doing what he loved day to day, but still energetic enough to take them on days out to theme parks. It's a testimony to his selflessness that he went on rollercoasters with them; he hated rollercoasters. But equal to that was his general interest in their lives, his practical advice and practical jokes, which in combination made him for Michael and Zoe the very best grandfather possible. The twins enjoyed seeing him. He had an unerring sense of the way to a child's heart: rude noises, sweets, pocket money. Despite his increasing infirmity, living close by, Polly, Freddie and Jessica had the opportunity to know him just as much as his other grandchildren – he was not a grandfather to miss out on.

'Finally, we come to Anne, his loving wife. One of the reasons my father would have been wrong to have chosen a life of a smallholder … it was as a policeman that he met Anne. It is no judgement on all the other people he loved and who loved him to say Anne made him happiest. It was partly her devotion to him, but she was also equal to his needs, whether that was helping him through his difficult relationship with his son, the daily chores of Beech Lodge, or, over these last five years, caring for him when illness took its toll. Over the decades Anne has been there, by his side, ready to challenge him when necessary, always to love him, and there is no doubt he lived longer through her love and devotion. And he knew it. In the end, a man wary of superstition, like many of us, came to believe Anne was not only wife, mother, grandmother, hairdresser, unqualified doctor, but was possibly an angel too. If anything was to restore his faith, lost at the death of his first wife and son, it was Anne.

'To finish: I doubt without Anne's energy and persistence they would have discovered Goa, a place that became a home from home, and where they made many friends, all devastated at the news of his passing. And I suspect, if we were to pop over to Goa and ask the locals about Mike Griffiths, they'd say the same as the locals of his beat, the players of all the teams he captained, his children and grandchildren – he was a huge presence when he was alive, but the hole he leaves in each of us will be greater still.'

I sit down. Bridget stills my hands, which are shaking.

The wake is tolerably short. People who knew him well for many years tell me that I've done him justice. Occasionally someone comes up and says, 'So you're Mike's boy then?'

'Yep,' I say. 'That's me.'

That night, I dream I am at his house and searching the cupboard for the shotgun I remember from my youth. Everywhere is empty. It's not even his house; it's large, cavernous, dusty. At one point it occurs to me my father's not dead; that the three weeks have passed and I need to put it right. But I can't find him. I do the next best thing: I wander the acreage shooting all the ducks and geese, standing over them at close range and pulling the trigger, *pow, pow, pow*. I stand alone in a world of floating white feathers.

Things Fall Apart II

To anyone who will listen in the next few weeks, I say, 'How is it that I wrote a eulogy for my father and could not think of, or bring myself to say, a single good thing about him from my own experience? It's funny, no?' I laugh out loud – *ha ha*. But I keep asking the question.

Anne and I drive up to the church and stand at the grave. She points to a bench she's bought and placed up against the church wall. We do not sit on it; it is for the summer, for shade. The grave is a long, low mound of thick clods of mud, flowers and wreaths, a temporary wooden cross; it is as well tended as it could possibly be at this stage. I cannot think of his big body under the turned earth. I can't picture him at all. It's like he's doubly gone: hidden by the earth and disappeared from my mind. I don't dare contemplate what this might mean. Have I been right all along: his death means a kind of freedom?

Between Christmas and New Year's Eve, thirteen of us walk over the fields to the village, cross the green to the church and stand around the grave. Again I feel nothing. I don't even have to pretend. Everyone assumes I feel what is normal; that I feel like they do. But the world is split now. There are those around the graveside that day, the three hundred people in the church a month or so ago, others around the country, around the world, and me. There are those who loved him, and there is me.

Over the next few months, what I say about my father, the stories I tell, are no different from those I've been telling for thirty years. They are pretty much word-for-word the same. The difference is that back then I thought I felt something, as if the facts were my feelings. But all I was doing was describing what happened in order to elicit a reaction in others, as if their feelings might stand in for my lack. But now, months after his death, I find myself acknowledging that I've never felt anything, then or now.

For some reason I stop the antidepressants. Bridget doesn't understand why, or why so suddenly and without guidance from my doctor. She becomes fearful of my moods and says she realises that she's been this way for a couple of years now. She describes my behaviour, the impatience, intolerance, the anger, and her need to anticipate how I might be ahead of time and adjust accordingly. There are times when our home is like the home of my childhood: my demand for quiet, my presence a thing to be wary of as much in its absence as when I am there, my mood the supreme governing entity.

There are differences, of course. As a family, they push back. Bridget tells me I'm being unreasonable, ignores me, carries on with what she is doing. Wilder calls me out and tries her best to explain what is wrong in what I say or do. Macleod can't cope with unfairness and points it out. In this sense we are more like the family next door to my childhood home – argumentative and noisy. There is also, for what it's worth, the fact that our house looks like the Yateses': cluttered, full of books, plants, vegetables I didn't recognise back then. But the repetition of what matters is intolerable to me. I hate myself. I hate him. He's not dead; he's alive and well, living inside me, stalking this house.

For days I feel weightless. For days I feel a gravitational pull downwards. For days I am like tidal water far from land. For days I crash relentlessly against rocks. I need to do something. Not seek help – do something. For various reasons, I have the idea to found a literary prize. I make it happen. It's not difficult. All my life I've known what it is to do: have an idea, make a plan, see it through. But the prize's success gives me no pleasure. After the first year, I basically give it away to someone else. Around the same time, my novel *As a God Might Be* is published. It is reviewed widely and to some acclaim. That gives me no pleasure either.

I realise something about myself. My whole life I've been looking for something that will transform me. Everything I've done has had one objective: change me. Whatever this transformational object might be – person, project, artwork – I've wanted it to lead me to myself, or provide a bridge over which I might walk to find the real me standing there, waiting. Except the bridge is the handiwork of a small boy with no strength and when I step out onto it, it collapses into the abyss. The enterprise has been futile from the beginning. And finally I know this.

Anne

A year after my father's death, Anne comes to London. I have booked an Italian restaurant that serves small bowls of pasta along a chrome bar. The moment she exits the station she asks how I am. The easy answer, *Good ... fine. How are you* catches in my throat; I can't bring myself to say it. Instead I confess, 'I don't know, Anne – things are bad.' She doesn't ask why, but I sense she hears me, wants to listen.

Sitting along the bar, our dishes and wine ordered, I turn to her. What do I say? There is so much. I start by telling her the story of that Christmas when I was depressed and he phoned to blame me for ruining Christmas for the grandchildren. I have no idea how she will respond. She says, 'He was a weak man.'

I drop my head into my hands; tears fill my palms and run down my wrists. A few feet away, across the bar, chefs are working, pan-frying ingredients a few inches above the flames, shuffling, tipping, sliding, making sure each ingredient is soft or golden or crisp, at which point they use tongs to lift out glistening pasta from large pans and dump it onto the sauces. The food is then shuffled into bowls lined up along the bar, with a half spin to signal the rapid elegance of execution.

I can't believe she has said this. I can't believe she has said *precisely* this.

The lunch lasts two hours and I can't stop crying. I try – I really do. I'm a fifty-three-year-old man who doesn't ordinarily cry, and we're in public, with young men only a few feet away. But I need to hear her. And it is in the saying of all these things out loud to her that it seems I finally feel what I've been saying for all these years. It breaks me.

I know I need to be careful. Anne's love for my father will be unwavering until she dies. She loved him like a saint, which is to say that as much as she believed in his saintliness, there was also something saintly in her love. I make sure she knows that I am pleased she and my father found each other; I understand how much she loved him and how happy they were. But she's not interested in that; she knows that. She wants me to talk. After each story her response is simple: 'Did he? That is wrong'; 'I'm sorry – he shouldn't have said that'; 'It wasn't your fault.' In this instant I love Anne as much as I've loved anyone. If anyone embodies what the wider world believed of my father it is her, and yet she is listening to me, comforting me without judgement. She doesn't try to defend him, because whatever I say, their life together will remain untouched. Yet that doesn't mean she doesn't believe what I am saying: that he was capable of such things. She manages to separate the fact of her love for him and the fuller truth, which includes how he treated me. I can see she is surprised by some of the things I say, but she is not shocked. It is all recognisable to her on some level. He wasn't an altogether different man with her over the thirty-plus years. Their happiness didn't change him. It is also the case that right now, to the person who loved my father most, I am more important than he is. This is what he must have felt for most of his life: one's own feelings to be the most important, for there to be no competition in care, attention, love. For the first time since the day I was born, my father has been set aside to make way for me.

After an hour, I apologise to the chefs working nearby – it must have been very off-putting, I say. I'm not sure they noticed.

Anne rests her hand on my forearm and says that based on this new information, she must move him out of Heaven and give him a spell in Purgatory. We both laugh. She also says I will need to forgive him if he is to be returned to God. I don't believe in any of these things, but I take some satisfaction from Anne's celestial demotion: it is an expression of how real what I've said is to her.

We leave the restaurant and walk to Charing Cross. I thank Anne over and over. I only now realise how close my life was to dangerously falling apart, and without her receptiveness, patience and kindness that day, I'm not sure whether I would have survived.

Truth

Things don't improve. The sense of slipping away remains. It's like a terrible seasickness or a large bolus of nothing rolling around in my gut, preparing itself to drop away into nothing. The structures of meaning I have inhabited for over fifty years are weakening. What Anne said about my father being a weak man was the first push against something holding me up, even though neither of us realised it at the time.

I am walking along the Embankment, from London Bridge to Tate Modern, to a reading by an author I will publish in a few years. Over the stone wall, the river is grey-black, churning and cold. Above the river, the sky is pure white, a sheet snapped tight. I am about halfway there when I take a swerve out of myself. Something from deep in my gut leaves me and flies away, over the river and up into the pure white sky. I can only describe it as feeling like the soul leaving the body after death or a kind of kenosis, a self-emptying in life. In an instant, all that is me has departed. Then I am back again. Only seconds have passed. Except that something isn't right. I am not the same as before; I have been disconnected from the world, as if my soul, having flown back in, has plunged too far down, dropped too far into the abyss, and what previously connected me to the world, some cord or thread, has snapped.

The sensation is not unfamiliar. There were those few days when I was sixteen, reading Proust, and suddenly felt separated from the world by a jellylike substance; then eight years later, when the world became a picture before me and I feared it would shatter at my feet. And other times when I've looked around and feared there was nothing to keep from falling away into nothingness, as if that were a step a person might take. But this is also different, a kind of doubling of the dissociative sensation. The world is now too real in its realness to be reached and I am too unreal in my unrealness to be reached. There is no way back.

I take the dogs for a walk in the small woods beside Tooting Athletics Track. It is on the edge of this wood, the dogs pulling to be let off their leads, that I sense the complete collapse of who I am. The dogs look up at me wondering what is happening, when I am going to release them. But I am not there. Or rather, I am thinking: *Where have I gone?* I am like a 1960s high-rise razed to the ground: one moment there and in seconds gone, a half-century of solidity dropped to the ground and dispersed into the air, leaving a quiet, dusty nothingness. You could walk through me. It doesn't matter that I am still standing and can't bend down to let the dogs off their leads, I have no internal structure, or only an after-image of who I once was, like a trace of light left on the eye … I have finally arrived at what I've known to be the case for most of my life. I am face to face with the abyss.

52–53 Years Old

In the beginning, there was a father and son, but the son was all of the father and none of himself, and because the son was the father and the father was gone, the son's world was without form, and void, and darkness was upon the face of the deep.

A Threadless Way

No more life.

No more life.

No more life.

This is what I keep saying to myself.

Forgive me, but I want to be precise. Let's say there is a line of lived experience, and at one end is joy in all its forms and at the other despair in its purest form. I contend that the depression I am describing cannot be found here, it cannot be plotted on this line, which is to say there is a kind of depression beyond despair. There is a psychiatric model for this, at least for mood, where Euphoria and Tension are represented at either end of the spectrum, suggesting that depression is categorically different. After all, depression is not the highest expression of Tension. Depression is not a state on the scale of feeling.

To live in good faith is to accept your life as your own, and as such, if you are offered the chance to live your life – the same life – over again, you will choose to live it exactly as was, with no alteration, variation or change. You will do this because you understand that you and your life are indissoluble, and therefore to want your life to be different, in whatever small way, is to want *not to be you*. But I am saying: no more life.

The darkness of the nothingness within me, the enlarging darkness, cannot be experienced as a feeling. It is one of the great contradictions of psychosis: I am numb and yet the mental anguish incapacitates me. There is no pain and yet it is unendurable. Only what can't be measured is the truth.

I am not in the world, but it cannot be said that I am in another place, because 'in' suggests a structure with*in* which one might exist, and no such structure exists. The experience of madness is to be in a logically impossible place and yet to look down and see one's body in the world going about its business.

I am a ghost, haunting myself.

It's in the body.

When I am lying in bed and Bridget turns a page of the book she is reading, when she strokes her thumb across the weave of the paper, creating the friction to gather it up to turn, the sound is thunderous in my ear, as if someone has got in there with some tiny instrument of torture. The traffic on the main road, a quarter of a mile away, is differently thunderous, as if there is a F1 race outside the house. If a car stops on the street and the driver leaves its engine running, the noise seems to rise from the road, enter the bedroom, surround me and shake me. I feel it personally. As if mysterious forces have decided to do this to me.

It's in the body.

The world cannot be otherwise. Nothingness is otherwise. The experience of nothingness is to know that it is possible to live otherwise. The *un*-fact in the world. The world persists: a noisy, cold place, without refuge.

Once nothingness has been encountered, you are in possession of the whole truth. This causes a kind of negative surprise. Think about it. You come face to face with the whole of the truth about the world, which is that there is a nothingness at its centre and into which all things can fall, and yet you still find yourself to be alive and going about your business.

I eat, walk the dogs, do laundry, write emails, cook for the children, watch TV.

'What do you *feel*? How does it make you *feel*?'

I have no feelings. I do not exist. Or rather: I do not exist, so how can I have feelings?

Your existence isn't real to me. Your subjectivity. Your agency. Your body. You in the light. You in the glare. The 3D you. The live-action you. If I don't exist then neither do you.

52–53 Years Old

How is it that we can know nothingness? What is it a percept of?

'And the earth was without form, and void; and darkness was upon the face of the deep.'

I am the abyss.

Part Eight

The Unconscious Has No Age

I

Over the next six months I tell Bridget, one or two friends, my doctor that I do not exist. I try to explain that this is not a hallucinatory state or delusion but the actual case. I use the tower block analogy. I quote the opening of the Book of Genesis, using my hands to shape a space disposed of content. Please believe this absence is real, the gesture implores.

They mustn't deny me this, I say, because it will cause a further erasure, a doubling of non-existence. It becomes clear to Bridget that if I am ever to come back from this, I can't do it alone. But I still refuse to see a therapist. Not because I believe I will out-think them but because I am now past saving. Then one afternoon, after walking the dogs, I collapse on the floor, or more precisely, it is as if my body, finally acknowledging its lack of internal structure, cannot keep me upright. I lie there for hours, with the sensation of the kitchen floor beneath me slowly giving way, and I am reminded of Kafka's Cossack, and wonder whether after forty years of mad dancing I have hollowed out the ground beneath me and my grave is taking shape.

Mark's consulting room was on the top floor of a fried chicken shop in London Bridge, a hundred yards down from Borough Market. I would arrive early, buy a cup of coffee, walk around the market trying the free samples of cheese, meats, bread. The act of eating was like a confirmation that I was present, but I was more like an animal grazing: instinctive, reflexive.

I always found myself at the gates to the building five minutes early and watched the time count down on my phone. The buzzer didn't always work properly, so I'd have to rattle the gates like a prisoner before the lock was released. The staircase up to the top floor was narrow, dark and fragrant; I think there was an aromatherapist somewhere in the building. Mark's room was bright, with two chairs, a couch, and a table with a small plant and a box of tissues. I sat in the chair by the door.

I spent weeks in that chair saying nothing. Mark didn't say anything either. But it wasn't a stand-off. He was content to wait. Saying nothing doesn't preclude speaking, of course. It remained the case, as it had been for much of my life, that I couldn't stop talking. I was full of ideas and theories. I'd claim to have untangled everything and found the solution to my problem.

Occasionally Mark would say: 'How does that make you feel?' And I'd be stumped. *Feel?* I'd think, *I don't feel anything.* And I'd say this or shake my head and move on. But he kept dropping the question in. Then at one point I wondered whether I'd ever felt anything, but that seemed impossible given the heightened states of emotion I'd been in for much of my life. Then one day I said maybe there is a real difference between emotion and feeling, and I'd spent my whole life showing the former but not experiencing the latter. In my case strong expressions of emotion were evidence of a lack of connection to feeling – the emotion was frustration. When I lost control, there was always a performative element, as if the feeling part of me was split off and I could watch what was happening with a kind of dispassion.

But what was happening now was different: there was no emotion either. While there had been times when I'd experienced a similar emptiness, even the possibility of the world itself shattering before me, this was happening *within* me – the lack of affect was mine, there was intentionality. But there is a chasm of difference between a lack of affect and a lack of intentionality. In the first I felt too little; in the second, there was no one to experience feelings.

Over the first few months of therapy, it seemed Mark's strategy was simply to be in the room with me. I think his aim was to prove I existed through *his* intentionality. It was one step at a time.

II

Why did object relations theory make the difference? I think that on some basic level it permitted me to look at my psychic development from a very young age and provide a way to think about the structure of my internal world.

The next question, I suppose, is why I found Fairbairn's model particularly persuasive. It started with his theory of the 'moral defence', a tendency in survivors of abuse to believe they are morally bad so that the 'caring object' – the perpetrator of the abuse – might be regarded as good, that the child needs to split off the bad behaviour of the abuser to maintain a relationship in an unsafe world, but because the child cannot deny the existence of the bad behaviour, it assigns the reason for the behaviour to itself. But what unlocked my particular problem further was Fairbairn's splitting of the parental carer into rejecting and enticing objects. Put simply: when the caregiver turns away they become a rejecting object, and because the infant wants them to turn back, they also become an enticing object.

This perfectly describes my relationship with my father. The easy part was his role as the rejecting object. While my father was still grieving, he couldn't connect with me, and my existence and Michael's death came to be entangled - I was a usurper taking the place of his first son and I was rejected. But then there is his role as the enticing object. He was a charismatic man and he can't be blamed for that, but this aspect of him was aided and abetted by my mother. From the earliest moments, I was taught that to have him as a father was a special privilege. His approval, his love, was everything.

I thought I'd escaped. For almost forty years I believed I'd built a life based on aspects of the world rejected by my father and that this made me categorically different from him, and therefore I could no longer be in his thrall. It was a neat solution. If he didn't possess the criteria to judge me, there was no need for me to try to prove myself, and if I didn't try to prove myself, nothing was being done for his approval. My swerve away from him, starting at the Yateses' house, and then made wonderfully real with my answer to Yossarian's question, meant that excluding a few conversations about cricket we shared no cultural touchpoints, and over time our relationship became one of duty – we were different people inhabiting different worlds. He never asked me about my world, and I seldom asked him about his.

Then one day, a year or so after his death, what became clear to me was that none of this had been true. I had been completely oblivious to my own behaviour. For the last forty years all I'd been doing was trying to prove myself to him. It might have been obvious to others, but I'd had no idea. A whole aspect of my behaviour was split off from me as I desperately acted it out. If you'd looked through the window you'd have seen it. Not my imagined 'I don't care what you think of me' but 'Can't you just find something in me to love?' The world I believed imaginary.

Then he died, and I realised that a dead person wasn't going to hear me, and it was in that moment I saw all the times I had tried to get him to take notice of me. It was like I was being forced to watch a showreel of highlights: in his garden, the lounge, dining room, me endlessly going on about what I was doing, the people I met, the projects I was working on, every one of my successes, however minuscule or irrelevant to him. I was insistent, incessant. But nothing ever turned his head. The enticing object and the rejecting object.

Later in life, girlfriends offered up the perfect opportunity to become both objects, and this goes a long way to explaining why I often became obsessed – to hold onto an Enticing object in the hope of being held back by it might have been what I'd have been after my whole life.

Six months after my father died, my body went into some kind of overdrive; I couldn't catch my breath, my gut was in spasm, there were weeks of dizziness, of disorientation. At night, hypervigilance kept me awake. Cascades of negative thoughts made my skin feel as if it was covered in a field of prickling electricity. Out of the house, my attention sought places of safety, where I thought that if I only lived there I'd feel secure. The sensation was mostly caused by a straightforward appearance of cosiness, a lamp on in a room in a house or flat. But I also looked at areas under trees and bushes, small and dark spots that I felt I could retreat into, hide and sleep. I was bringing the unconscious into the body: what I had previously experienced as deprivation was now being felt by my nervous system, and I was being alerted to more direct concerns about my safety. It was as if I realised this was what had always been at stake.

For some people, the depth and power of damaging internal relationships can persist indefinitely, even after the death of the originating objects. The battle never ceases. In this way I was lucky. In dying, my father not only left the building, he also took the foundations with him, and there were no other object relations in my unconscious to keep me going. In this sense there was a double loss: I was deprived of the deprivations, which explains the extent of the emptiness. But now what?

I needed a good object. Fairbairn's model doesn't include this, but I think that's his point: the good object doesn't reside in our unconscious, it must remain outside, and perhaps it isn't an object at all but an emergent property between two people.

Sitting in that chair above the chicken shop, I realised what Mark had been doing all along. He was making sure he gave me no reason to take him in as another rejecting object. Or, stated more positively, he was going to show me that a good object can exist in the world. And if I was willing, I might accept that there was someone in the world whom I could trust.

III

I do not blame my mother and father for wanting another baby. It's what couples did back then. I suppose the real question is whether they had a choice in how they related to me once they made that decision. Rather than the simple, expected happiness brought by a new baby, could they have acknowledged the inevitable emotional complexity that was going to be present at my birth, and that as family we would always have this shadow over us, and that whatever they might have wanted from me – a tiny, hours-old baby – there was no escaping this? I suppose I am asking whether, had it been possible for my parents to allow their sorrow to be part of our family life, we might have endured it together and helped one another through. But this would have required my parents setting aside their needs. Winnicott talks about a mother's 'willingness [...] to drain interest from her own self on to the baby', and then this devastating passage: 'There are two kinds of maternal disorder that affect this issue. At one extreme is the mother whose self-interests are too compulsive to be abandoned, so that she fails to plunge into the extraordinary condition. [...] At the other extreme is the mother who tends to be preoccupied in any case, and the baby becomes her *pathological* preoccupation'. (Italics in the original.) Looking back, my mother was both extremes: her self-interest was completely enmeshed with my father's, which meant she was pathologically preoccupied with her baby as a version that was going to be right *for him*. And my father's presence structured the household so completely that survival required us to drain interest from ourselves onto him. My mother had twenty-two years of life before meeting my father. She also had forty-four years of life after him. And over those years with him, it was her choice to drain interest from herself onto him. It was offered to me as the only way to live.

We are – sort of – at the end. Three years after my father's death, my mother died. If there are good and bad deaths, hers was bad: pancreatic cancer in a care home during the first Covid-19 lockdown, with no visitors allowed during her last four weeks, although my sister stood outside the care home window every day for an hour. But it had been a bad *dying* before then; her life coming to an end seemed to confuse her, something wasn't adding up. When she looked around her small bungalow she was asking herself *Is this it?*, because on some level she still believed it was supposed to have been different, she had deserved more, some version of herself she had glimpsed on holiday in Naples in the late 1950s. Her last few months were almost intolerable. Her GP and community nurse both refused to investigate complaints of a blockage when she couldn't hold food down, and instead prescribed her higher doses of anti-nausea medication, driving her to the point of despair and an attempt on her own life. It was only when she was taken to hospital and vomited in front of the doctor that she was scanned and a blockage was found. It was too late; she'd been driven mad. She died alone, confused and unhappy.

I wrote the eulogy easily. I realised I understood her and could write with honesty, from me to her. It was, in its way, the closest we'd been for almost forty years. Twelve people were allowed at the service, and much of the organisation was handled by Toni. I cried delivering the eulogy; I felt what I said about her in the allotted three minutes to sum her up in her simple complexity: she wanted more than life gave her, and that perhaps we have that in common. I am not sure what this tells me. Perhaps I loved her, although I am not convinced. Like my father, she now doesn't seem real, and I seldom think of her. It would be over-simplistic to say that I was parentless my whole life so nothing much had changed, but I think that's part of it. I have seen how friends are affected by the deaths of their parents, and whatever difficulties there might have been between them, they seemed to have something real to mourn. In the terms we've been using, we might call this the presence of that ultimate good object, shared love.

On the third anniversary of my father's death, we – Bridget and the twins, Anne, Clare and her children, all the dogs – met at his graveside. We stood awkwardly, remarked on its upkeep. I looked around at recent burials, the long mounds of churned, claggy mud, temporary crosses dug in. Anne said a prayer, reading from a small slip of paper. We then went for a three-hour walk. He wasn't mentioned, or only in passing, as we chatted about this or that, which is to say: he wasn't talked *about*. Maybe the others were being polite; I am sure they missed him terribly. But there was nothing for me to miss. Whatever there had been had disappeared.

Maybe sometimes the abyss has its uses.

Acknowledgements

Katherine Angel read the first version of this memoir during lockdown and her notes were generous, playful, tough. She then read the penultimate version in 2025 and doubled down on toughness. This book wouldn't be what it is without her hard work and seriousness of intent.

Without Damian Lanigan's support I would have never completed the penultimate version. His focus on what was required never wavered. His notes of encouragement kept me going.

A lot of important people in my life aren't featured or named, but their support and patience of the last forty-five years requires acknowledging. In no particular order: Louise Moulton, Tessa Thornley and her parents, Clare Moses, Neil Partrick, Kam Raslan, George Young, Luke Meddings, Tamsin Meddings, Emmanuelle Keita, Paul and Ondine Barrow, Marcus Wright, Linda Barton, Amanda Lane, John Scanlan, Kate Moran, Darren Rogers, Chris Bacher, Richard and Dian Macauley, my colleagues at Blinc, Leo Hollis, James Tookey, Brian Libby, Lamorna Ash, Elizabeth Oldfield, Jim Poyser, Rebecca Abrams, Alice Jolly, Sam Mills, and my dogs, who've both now gone, Django and Wolfie.

Of named people, special thanks and love to Bridget, Wilder and Macleod, who have had to put up with an awful lot over the decades. Valarie Smith for being my most cherished reader. Mark Vernon, a Good object if there ever was one.

Thank you to the Centre of Freudian Analysis and Research – especially Dr Andrew Hodgkiss, whose lecture on Lacan's mirror phase supplied the insight on the transmission of the paternal function that I required to make sense of this whole story.

And then there is the production. Thank you to Thomas Harding for taking the photograph in Paris that winter, Luke Bird for the elegant design, James Tookey (again) for typesetting, Toby Culff and CMP for finally making printing frictionless, Sarah Terry, copy editor, who always makes an unquantifiable positive difference to all our books, Clem Clement for proofreading, and all at Turnaround.

THE WRONG SON

NEIL GRIFFITHS

First published in 2026
by Weatherglass Books

A CIP record for this book is published by the British Library

ISBN: 978-1-0681766-9-2

Cover design: Luke Bird
Typesetting: James Tookey

Printed in the U.K. by CMP Books, Dorset

www.weatherglassbooks.com

Weatherglass
Books